蘇州舊住宅

SUZHOU VERNACULAR DWELLINGS

陳從周

目录 | Table of Contents

苏州位于江苏省东南部，周代时为吴国都城，后来三国两晋仍以"吴"称，至北宋政和年间改称"平江府"，元为"平江路"，明属江南省称"苏州府"，入清仍旧。当时，苏州有吴、长洲、元和三县，到民国则统名为"吴县"。1949 年后，成立苏州市，范围包括城区及近郊。四郊属吴县。

苏州旧住宅，规模大小不同者，在今日存留下来的数量很多，苏州在研究中国住宅建筑中是个重要地区。1957 年春，建筑工程部建筑科学院带领大家调查全国旧住宅，我们是以华东为重点，苏州是其中重要地区之一。几年来，我们调查了数百处，进行测绘、摄影的共 50 余处，就所得资料，编《苏州旧住宅参考图录》一书并写成此文。限于著者的水平，不妥的地方尚请读者指正。

Located in southeast part of Jiangsu province, Suzhou served as the capital of Wu State (吴国) during Zhou (周 circa 1100 BC–256 BC) dynasty. The name Wu was used through the Three Kingdoms (三 国 220–280) and both West and East Jin (两晋 265–420) dynasties. It was renamed to Pingjiang Fu (平江府) during Zhenghe period (政 和 1111–1118) of North Song (北 宋 960–1127) dynasty. The city was once again reamed during Yuan (元 1206–1368) dynasty to Pingjiang Lu (平 江 路), and then, Suzhou Fu of Jiangnan Province (江南省) during Ming (明 1368–1644) and Qing (清 1616–1911) dynasties. Suzhou was composed of the counties of Wu, Changzhou, and Yuanhe (吴、 长 洲、 元 和). After the founding of Republic of China in 1912, they merged into Wu County. The City of Suzhou was formed after the establishment of People's Republic of China in 1949, and it includes downtown and surrounding suburbs. The remaining rural areas fall under the jurisdiction of Wu County.

Great quantities of Suzhou's residence of various sizes and styles have survived up to present (1950s). This area played an important role in research of Chinese residential architecture. The Institute of Architecture Science of the Ministry of Architecture and Construction led an effort to study traditional Chinese residences during spring of 1957. Our work was focused on the eastern China area with emphasis in the Suzhou area. During these years we investigated several hundred sites. Over fifty of them were surveyed with plots and photographs. We compiled the materials collected in to the book *Pictures and Figures of Traditional Suzhou Residences* (《苏州旧住宅参考图录》). This article was written during that time. Any corrections or suggestions for this book are welcomed.

Natural Environment

Suzhou is geographically located on the south side of Yantze River delta, at 120° 37′ east longitude, 31° 17′ north latitude. It reaches Wusong River (吴淞江) on the east, borders Taihu Lake (太湖) on the west. It is easily accessible to Yangtze River on the north and Hangzhou, Jiaxing and Huzhou on the south. The downtown occupies an area of fourteen square kilometers. Mo Dan (莫旦), a poet of Ming dynasty, described Suzhou in his *Prose of Suzhou* (《苏州赋》) that Suzhou is directly controlled by the central government, and occupies the upstream in Jiangsu and Zhejiang provinces . This indicates the importance of the city. The city benefits greatly from river-based transportation through crisscrossing waterways in the city. The oceanic weather pattern provides a temperate and moist climate. There is no severe winter or summer in this area, but during the prolonged rain season known as Meiyu (梅雨, plum rain), it could be extremely humid. The highest temperature can reach 41 °C in summer, and the lowest point may reach –12 °C in winter. The average annual rainfall is approximately 1,048 millimeters with forty percent concentrated during summer months and eleven percent in the winter, which makes it an area with the most evenly spread out rainfall through out the year in the country. The monsoon in spring, Meiyu in summer, typhoon in fall, and vortex in winter all contribute to the annual rainfall. The wind direction varies from southeast in the summer to northwest in the winter. The winter is relatively mild averaging about three to four days of frosting per year. During summer the hot season may last forty-seven days. Sunny days account for over thirty percent of the year, over fifty percent of which is in July and August. The houses tend to face south

自然条件

苏州位于长江三角洲的南部，位居东经120° 37′，北纬31° 17′的地方，东通吴淞江，西邻太湖，北通长江，南达杭嘉湖，城区面积达14平方千米。明代莫旦《苏州赋》所谓"苏州拱京师以直隶，据江浙之上游"，可以想见其位置重要了。城内河道纵横，水路交通很是便利。气候属海洋性，因为受海风的滋润影响，所以气候温和湿润，无严寒酷暑，不过梅雨期较长，甚感湿闷。全年温度最高为41摄氏度，最低为零下12摄氏度。全年雨量在1048毫米左右，40%集中在夏季各月，冬季各月的雨量亦达全年11%，成为我国地理环境中雨量最匀润的区域。雨量的分布以春季的季风雨、夏季的梅雨、秋季的台风雨和冬季的气旋雨为最重要。风向，夏季多东南风，冬季多西北风。冬季不太冷，冻期仅3~4天；夏季温度较高，炎热期达47天之多。全年平均日照率在30%以上，七、八两月在50%以上。因此，在这种自然条件之下，房屋朝向多南向与东南向；房屋建筑高度较高，进深较大；屋顶用草架施覆水椽（双层屋顶）以资防热；平面上尽可能用前后天井；门窗都用长槅扇（落地长窗）及低槛窗。在夏季，北向房屋是尤为凉爽的地方；所以，倒座及北向的厅事均有其存在之必要。土壤属黏土，其上覆有机土与人工堆积土，单位承载量每平方米为10~12吨。附近太湖诸山及金山等地皆产石，陆墓（慕）御窑等地产砖，建筑材料除木材仰给于他省如福建、江西、湖广等外，一部分若银杏、枸树等木材本地亦有之，然为数不多。农产品以水稻为主，鱼、虾、水果产量亦丰富。

社会背景

"上有天堂，下有苏杭"，这是说明在封建社会时苏州是一个繁华与富庶的地方。当然，之所以形成上述情形，除自然方面的土地肥沃、气候温和与农业发达外，社会因素也是很重要的。

or southeast with increasing height and depth. A double-roof frame known as Caojia (草架 , rough frame) is used to prevent heat. The plan structure is constructed with front and rear courtyards, long lattice doors, and low sill windows to provide good insulation and ventilation. The north facing rooms are especially cool during summer. This makes reverse seated buildings (倒座) and north facing halls a necessity. The soils are mostly clay with a mix of organic soil and man-made dirt on top. The unit weight bearing capacity of soil is at ten to twelve metric tons per square meter. The construction materials are supplied from different areas. Rocks are provided by the neighbouring Taihu lake region and Jinshan Hill. Bricks are produced in Yuyao, Lumu , where an imperial kiln was located. The sources of wood supply are mainly from Fujian, Jiangxi, and Huguang (Hunan and Hubei) provinces. The local area can only provide a limited amount of lumber. The main agriculture product in this region is rice, and there is an abundant yield of fresh-water fish, shrimp, and fruit.

Social Conditions

The saying that there is a paradise in the heaven, and Su Hang on the earth (" 上有天堂，下 有 苏 杭 ". Su and Hang here means Suzhou and nearby Hangzhou in Zhejiang province) reflects the prosperity of Suzhou during feudalistic periods of China. In addition to a favorable natural environment including rich soil, temperate climate, and a well-developed agriculture, the human and social conditions play a very important role in its development.

Suzhou has developed its handicraft industry and economy since the period of Wu State in Zhou dynasty through Qin (秦 221 BC–207 BC) and

Han (汉 206 BC–220 AD) dynasties and the Three Kingdoms period, Suzhou became very prosperous during the Six Dynasties (六朝 222–589) period. The opening of Great Canal (运河 pronounced as Yunhe) which passed through Suzhou starting in Sui (隋 581–618) dynasty, and the development of foreign trade from Tang (唐 618–907) dynasty had contributed to the development of business and handicrafts in Suzhou area. During the Five Dynasties (五代 907–960) period, Suzhou was part of the Wuyue State (吴越国), which was not affected by the warfare. This made it possible for Suzhou to maintain the prosperity and growth. The city was named Pingjiang Fu during Song dynasty and Emperor Zhao Gou (Gaozong reigned from 1127–1162) once stayed here when he had a visit around the country. The city had a sizable business and industry during Song dynasty. The city planning shown in the *Map of Pingjiang* (drawn in 1229 or 2nd year of Shaoding period during Song dynasty) as well as wood structure buildings constructed during that period such as the Sanqingdian (built in 1179, or 6th year of Chunxi period during Song dynasty) of Xuanmiaoguan (also known as Tianqingguan) further demonstrates the prosperity of the time. In the *Story of Zhang's Garden and Pavillion in Lingbi* (《灵璧张氏园亭记》), Su Shi wrote: "The large halls are as elengant and subtle as those of Wu and Shu." It shows the advanced skills of Suzhou's construction crews. Jiangsu and Zhejiang were the only two provinces that were prosperous during Yuan dynasty, which enabled them to maintain the economy and to construct new large residences. The Jiangnan Province in early Ming dynasty were one of the richest regions in the nation. Since mid Ming dynasty, the city economy tended to be more and more prosperous, and many

苏州从周代的吴国以后，经秦、汉、三国，在经济及手工业技术方面不断地发展与提高，到六朝已成为富庶的地区。隋代运河畅通后，苏州又是其经过的地方，兼以唐以后的海外贸易，都促使了商业与手工业的发展。苏州五代时属吴越，因未曾加入中原的兵戈，维持了它的小康局面，在经济方面仍是繁荣。宋称"平江府"，赵构（高宗）曾驻跸于此。以宋代的经济来看，其时的城市工商业相当可观，《平江图》（1229年，宋绍定二年）所示城市规划与玄妙观（宋称"天庆观"）的三清殿（1179年，宋淳熙六年）木构建筑都可以证明。苏轼《灵璧张氏园亭记》所说"华堂夏屋有吴蜀之巧"，足证其时苏州建筑技术的成就。元代，唯江浙两省为富庶，致使其经济仍能维持，因此尚有足够财力营建规模较大的住宅。进入明代的江南省，财务尤为全国之冠；中叶后，城市经济日趋繁荣，而退休官僚即于此置田构宅、经营商业，终老苏州。土地兼并日甚一日，对劳动人民剥削更渐趋加重，至清代仍继续着。拥有这样大量的旧式住宅及园林建筑的地方，在今日全国除北京外要首推苏州了。

苏州是一个手工业与消费的城市，手工业制作精湛。过去居住者，一类是地主官僚；一类是手工业劳动者；一类是代地主官僚经营或自己经营的商人，其中利润最大的有钱庄、酱园、典当、银楼等行业。地主官僚除本地的外，他处羡慕苏州繁华而移居其地的亦很多，尤以浙北皖南人为最多。浙北的如海宁陈姓、吴兴沈姓、嘉兴王姓等。皖南以旧徽州府而论，如潘、程、汪、曹诸大姓皆为明代后移入。徽州人喜置第宅，今苏州旧式大住宅大都属以上诸姓，似乎亦有此原因。在地主官僚、商人层层剥削下，住宅有着极明显的阶级性。一种是大第宅，属大地主、大官僚与富商所有；另一种较小者，属中小型地主官僚所有，或一般业主所有。至于手工业者及商店职工，则租赁地主官僚等所建

retired aristocrats preferred to buy fields, construct residences, operate business and live in Suzhou for their old ages. But on the other hand many lands were consolidated by the rich and the labouring people were severely exploited by the land owners. Land consolidation continued till Qing dynasty. This may explain why this area has such a large collection of traditional residences and gardens second only to the City of Beijing.

Handicraft and commerce are two vital industries in Suzhou. The craftsmanship in Suzhou is especially exquisite. In the past, residents of the city were mainly composed of artistocrats, handicraft makers and artisans, businessmen and their agents. The banks, sauce and pickle shops, pawn shops, and silverware shops were the most profitable among various businesses operated in Suzhou. This group of people included the local aristocrats as well as many who admired the prosperity of Suzhou and relocated from northern Zhejiang and southern Anhui provinces. The major surnames such as Chen from Haining, Shen from Wuxing, and Wang from Jiaxing etc are all from northern Zhejiang province. And the surnames of Pan, Cheng, Wang, and Cao all migrated to Suzhou from southern Anhui province in the old Huizhou Fu area after Ming dynasty. The people form Huizhou Fu region liked to build large residences, thus people from this region constructed most of the large residences existing in Suzhou today. The differences of these houses reflect the different classes of the owners. The large residences, for instance, were typically owned by major land owners, or aristocrats, or rich businessmen; the medium sized for mid level aristocrats. The craftsmen, artisans, and store clerks typically rent small houses built by the large real estate owners. In late 1800s and early 1900s, newly rising industrialists took some of the large residences that were once owned by the aristocrats.

The publication of *Yingzao Fashi* (《营造法式》, Methods of Construction) during South Song dynasty in Suzhou area had a significant impact on architectural design and construction in the region. The craftsmen of nearby Xiangshan and Mudu area had worked on the design and construction of palaces of both Nanjing and Beijing during Ming dynasty. Kuai Xiang, a famous architect at that time, was from Xiangshan region. In addition, there were several architecture books including *Yuanye* (《园冶》) by Ji Cheng, *Changwuzhi* (《长物志》) by Wen Zhenheng, *Yijiayan* (《一家言》) by Li Yu, *Gongduan Yingzao Lu* (《工段营造录》) by Li Dou, as well as *Yingzao Fayuan* (《营造法原》) by Yao Chengzu of late Qing dynasty. These books all had significant impacts either directly or indirectly on the development of architecture design and construction techniques in the region. In the mean time, the craftsmanship and cultural advances contributed to the continuous development of architecture.

The design and construction of these buildings reflect social conditions, material foundation, and economic situation of the period. They illustrate the wisdom of the craftsman, and builders. These buildings are a very important part of our cultural heritages. They are also valuable sources of information for those who study the history of architecture, residential buildings, and sociology.

的极其简陋的房屋。到清末民国初，新兴的资本家又代替一部分没落的地主官僚而占有大住宅了。

《营造法式》自南宋绍兴年间重刊于平江，对苏州建筑起了一定的推动作用。进入明代，其附近香山木渎的匠人参加了两京宫殿营建，如著名的建筑家蒯祥即香山人。至若计成的《园冶》、文震亨的《长物志》、李渔的《一家言》、李斗的《工段营造录》，以及清末姚承祖《营造法原》等，都对住宅建筑直接或间接地在设计与技术方面起了推进作用。手工业与文化的发达给予住宅建筑在原有基础上得以提高的有利条件。

这些住宅的设计与建造充分地反映了当时的时代背景、物质及经济基础。此外，劳动人民更在建筑方面呈现了无比的智慧，他们遗留下的这一批珍贵遗产是值得我们继承的。除去为建筑史与住宅建筑提供资料外，对社会科学方面的研究亦是一份宝贵的资料。

苏州住宅区鸟瞰图
Bird's-eye view of residential area

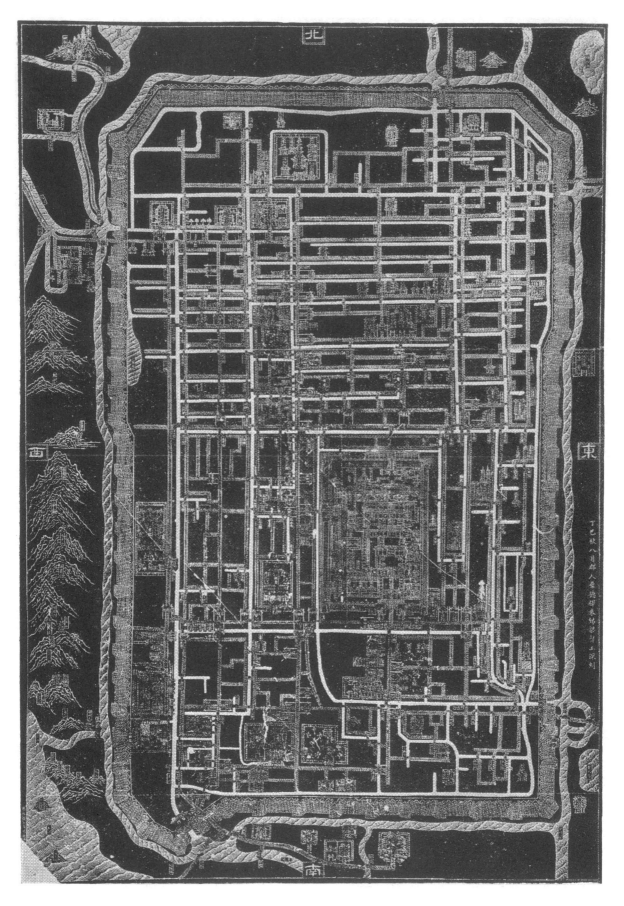

北

西

東

南

丁巳秋八月郡人葉逵輯重摹繪并工深刊

14

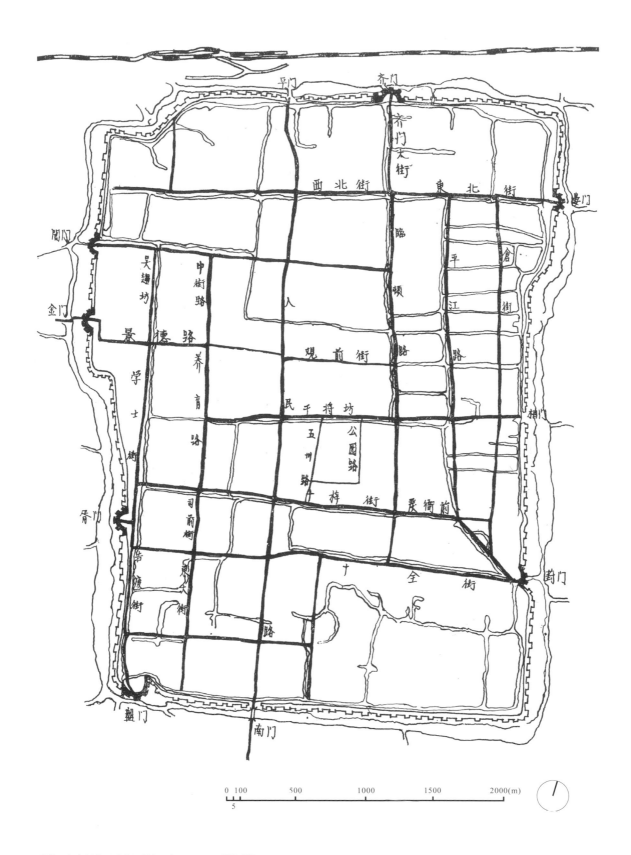

上：苏州瑞光塔附近旧城
下：悬桥巷巷景

Top: Area near Ruiguang Pagoda
Bottom: View of Xuanqiao Lane

上：盘门水城门
下：盛家浜住宅

Top: Water gate of Gate Pan
Bottom: Residences at Shengjiabang

上：大儒巷潘宅天井
下：天官坊陆宅贴砖墙

Top: Courtyard of Pan's residence at Daru Alley
Bottom: Brick-covered wall of Lu's residence at Tianguan Fang

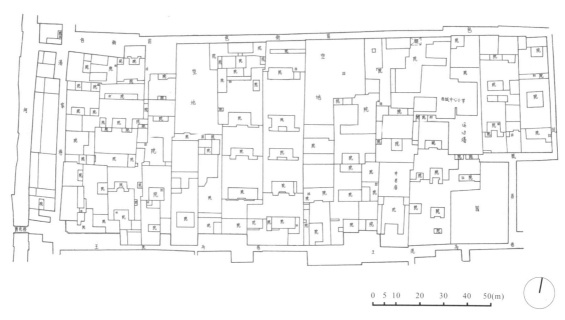

本页上：苏州部分旧居住区图
本页下：阔街头巷网师园道古轩（又名"小山丛桂轩"）
对页：阔街头巷网师园园门入口

汤家巷陆宅　南向，平面曲尺形。大门从东入，为一小天井。主屋面阔二间，一为起居室，一为住屋，其西首系一小厢。楼梯与厨房在主屋后，无后天井。二楼平面与一层同。

蒲林巷吴宅　系词曲家吴梅故居。南向，入门门屋一间，折西为楼厅与两厢组成三合院，从厅东首小门可导至书斋，斋仅一间，前后列天井，是利用门屋后隙地建造的。厅后为上房楼屋五间，天井中东侧有一月门可通至书斋后天井。披屋（即下房）、厨房皆在上房后。此宅用地不多，颇为适用。

Lu's residence at Tangjia Alley is a south facing residence with an L-shaped floor plan. A small courtyard follows the main gate opening to the east side. The main building is two-bay wide. One bay is used as the living room, and the other as the bedroom. An annex (Xiang or 厢 which means either wings or annexes) connects to the west side. The stair and kitchen are behind the main house, but there is no rear courtyard. The floorplan of the second floor is identical to that of the first floor.

Wu's residence at Pulin Alley used to be the residence of Wu Mei, an expert on traditonal Chinese opera. This south facing racidence has a lobby after the main gate. On the west side of the lobby a two-story hall with two wings form a Sanheyuan (courtyard with houses on three sides, see section and floor plan for description of these complex) compound. The small door on east side of the house opens to a study that is one bay wide. The front and rear courtyard to the study is built on remaining space behind the lobby area. A main house that is five bays wide follows the hall and a small moon gate on the east side of main house courtyard opens to rear courtyard of study. The servants' room (披 屋 pronounced as Piwu) and the kitchen are all located behind the main house. This house is quite compact and effecient.

对页上：汤家巷陆宅一层、二层、屋顶平面图（由左至右）
对页中：蒲林巷吴宅一层、二层平面图（由左至右）
对页下：蒲林巷吴宅剖面图
Opposite top: Ground, first floor and roof plans of Lu's residence at Tangjia Alley (from left to right)
Opposite middle: Ground and first floor plans of Wu's residence at Pulin Alley (from left to right)
Opposite bottom: Section of Wu's residence at Pulin Alley

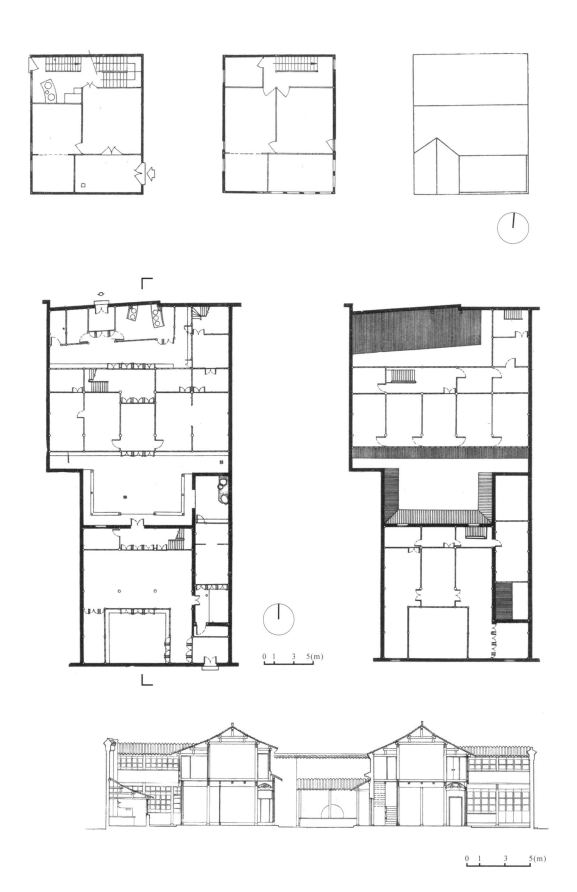

0 1   3   5(m)

0 1   3   5(m)

21

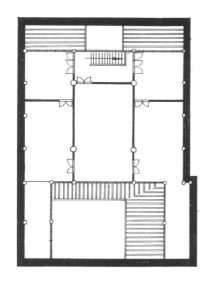

甲

马大篆巷张宅 平面为一"H"形，楼厅三间，翼以前后厢房，门屋系利用东厢，后天井之东厢即作为厨房。此种形式，江南称为"四盆一汤"式。此类小型住宅天井之外墙端往往开瓦花墙（即瓦砌漏窗），或置琉璃预制漏窗以便通风采光。

Zhang's residence at Madalu Alley has an H-shaped floor plan. A three-bay wide two-story hall has two side houses both in front of and behind it. The front east side house is used as lobby. The rear east side house is used as kitchen. This style of residence is called Sipenyitang (Four Dishes and One Soup) style in Jiangnan region. The exterior walls in this type of residence have lattice windows made from tile or porcelain to enhance lighting and air flow.

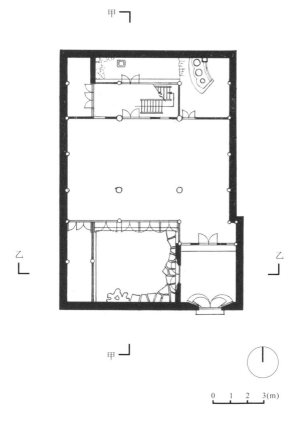

乙　　　　　　　　　　　乙

甲

0　1　2　3(m)

上：马大篆巷张宅二层平面图
下：马大篆巷张宅一层平面图

Top: First floor plan of Zhang's residence at Madalu Alley
Bottom: Ground floor plan of Zhang's residence at Madalu Alley

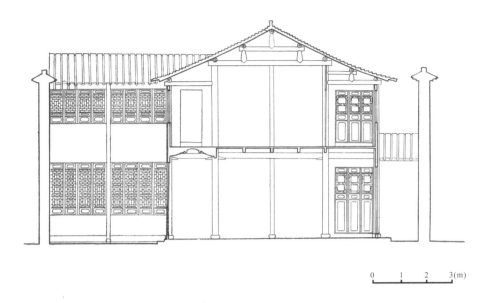

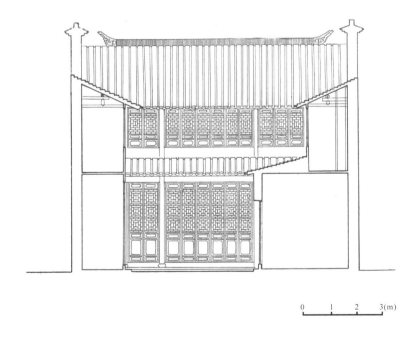

上：马大簏巷张宅剖面图 甲—甲
下：马大簏巷张宅剖面图 乙—乙

Top: Section of Zhang's residence at Madalu Alley 甲—甲
Bottom: Section of Zhang's residence at Madalu Alley 乙—乙

阔街头巷张宅　此为苏州著名园林网师园之住宅部分，清乾隆年间为宋宗元宅，后归嘉定瞿远村，同光年间属李鸿裔，民国后归张锡銮、何亚农。叶公绰、张善子、张大千皆曾分居其园宅。是宅大门外尚存大型照壁，东西辕门，为今日苏州住宅中大型照壁的硕果仅存者。大门外石板路修整，照壁前植柏树盘槐，树池外衬以冰裂纹铺地，雅洁自然，与前者适成严谨与活泼之对比。大门抱鼓石、门簪、高槛俱在。入门进轿厅，西折为网师园，但见回廊片段，与处于前后假山间的小山丛桂轩。轩西北有曲廊，折北为濯缨水阁，北向。其前为池，池西侧筑六角亭，缀以游廊，向前至西北转角处有曲桥。桥北看松读画轩，面阔四间，三间南接山石，西端一间置小院。轩东临水，有廊名"射鸭"，其后筑楼，东又以一楼贯之，盖即在女厅后者。轿厅后为大厅、女厅（上房），皆在一中轴线上。大厅面阔三间，旁列书斋。女厅系楼厅，面阔六间，

Zhang's residence at Kuojietou Alley is the residential section of the famous Suzhou garden Wangshi Garden (the Master-of-Nets Garden). This was the residence of Song Zhongyuan during Emperor Qianlong (乾隆) of Qing dynasty. Its owner became Qu Yuancun of Jiading (嘉定) region, and later by Li Hongyi. After the founding of Republic of China in 1912, Zhang Xiluan and later He Yalong owned this residence. Ye Gongzhuo, Zhang Shangzhi, and Zhang Daqian all lived in part of this residence at one time. A large Zhaobi (a decorative structure, known as 照壁 in Chinese), and both east and west Yuanmen (辕门, outer gate) still exist. This is the only large scale Zhaobi that exists in Suzhou today. The stone slab road outside the main gate is orderly paved. There are cypress and Chinese scholar trees planted in front of the Zhaobi. The tree well is coupled with ice break pattern making it natural and elegant. This contrast with the structured and serious scene formed by Zhaobi and cypress tree. The drum shaped base stones, door pegs, and thresholds are all well preserved. Jiaoting (roughly means carriage or sedan hall) follows the main gate. The west side is Wangshi Garden where a small section of circular corridor is viewable along with the Xiaoshanchongguixuan (a veranda called 小山丛桂轩 in Chinese) that is located between two hillocks. There is a winding corridor on the northwest of the veranda, and a north facing water pavilion to its north. A pond is in front of the water pavilion. A six-sided pavilion is to the west side of the pond and a viewing corridor adorns the scene. A winding bridge is found at the northwest corner of the passage. The Kansongduhuaxuan (a veranda called 看松读画轩 in Chinese) is north of the bridge. This structure is four bays wide. Three bays are connected to hillocks, and the fourth bay has a small courtyard attached. There is a corridor facing the water to the east side of this Xuan that is called Sheya. A building is built behind this corridor, and another building is built to the east side. This last structure is right behind the Nüting (masters' house). Both the main hall and Nüting are located behind Jiaoting along the central axis. The main hall is three bays wide with a study on the side. Nüting is a two-story building that is six bays wide. Five bays are visible and one is hidden with a wing connected to the east side. The courtyard is wide rectangle shaped enclosed by lattice-windowed short walls on the sides and osmanthus trees inside. This is where the ladies stay during warm summer days. The building behind the Sheya corridor acts as transition between the garden and residence section. The whole garden can be seen from the top of this structure, which features this residence. The kitchen and servants' houses are all located beyond the main houses.

The next case is **Zhang's residence at Xiuxian Alley**. Zhang family was a rich land owner, and businessman from Nanxun (南 浔) region in Zhejiang. This was their temporary residence when visiting Suzhou. The main buildings consist of only one gate house, Jiaoting and masters' house. All of the structures are three bays wide. There is an exquisite Huating (flower hall) that is three bays wide to the east. Two wings are located both in front and behind the flower hall. The area in front of the hall was increased in this fashion. Taihu Lake rocks, osmanthus, and Chinese parasol trees were planted in front of the hall making it an enchanting and quiet scene. This is where the guests were entertained. There is a small hall that is carpenter's square shaped (also known as L shaped) located directly hehind the flower hall. A building used as pawn shop is located further to the north. The majority of this building has been destroyed. This pawn shop faces to the north, and its entrance is facing the main street, Jingde Road.

明五暗一, 东首联厢, 天井为横长方形, 两侧隔以短垣, 上列漏窗, 内植桂树, 为女眷夏日纳凉之处。射鸭廊后一楼为园宅之过渡, 登楼可俯视全园, 为此宅之一重要特征。厨房下房均在正屋之后。

修仙巷张宅 张氏为浙江南浔的地主富商, 此屋为其来苏停居之所, 因此主要建筑物仅门屋、轿厅与楼厅（上房）各一座, 皆面阔三间。其东置一精致的三间花厅, 厅后置左右二厢, 俾厅前面积增大。厅前置湖石, 植桐桂, 皆楚楚有致, 极为幽静, 为主人会宾的地方。花厅后尚有一小厅作曲尺形。再北为典当房, 今损毁已大半。当房北向, 正门由大街景德路出入。

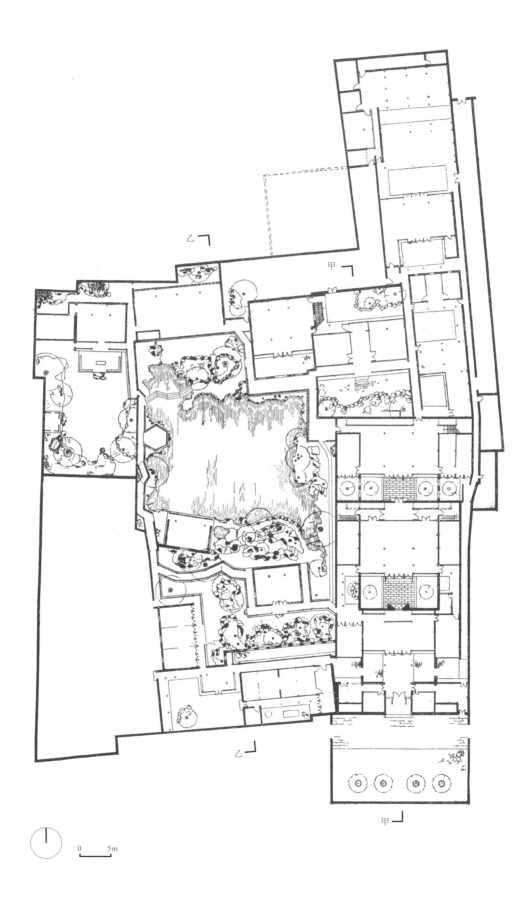

乙

甲

乙

甲

0　　5m

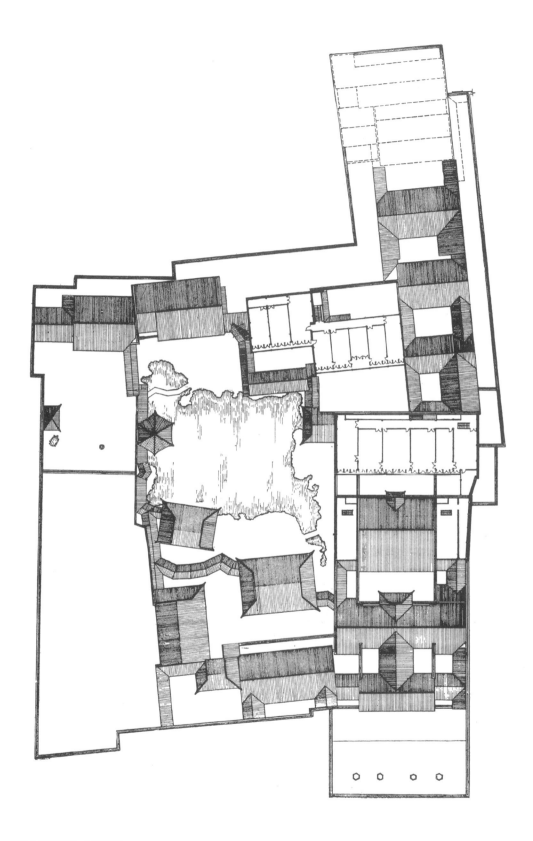

对页：阔街头巷网师园一层平面图
本页：阔街头巷网师园二层平面图

Opposite: Ground floor plan of Wangshi Garden
This page: First floor plan of Wangshi Garden

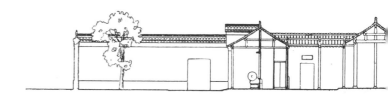

本页上：阔街头巷网师园自住宅俯视园池
对页上：阔街头巷网师园楼厅
中：阔街头巷网师园住宅剖面图 甲—甲
下：阔街头巷网师园剖面图 乙—乙

This page top: Overlook of Wangshi Garden with water pool
Opposite top: Stories hall of Wangshi Garden
Middle: Section of living area of Wangshi Garden 甲 – 甲
Bottom: Section of the park of Wangshi Garden 乙 – 乙

0 1 3 5(m)

0 1 2 3(m)

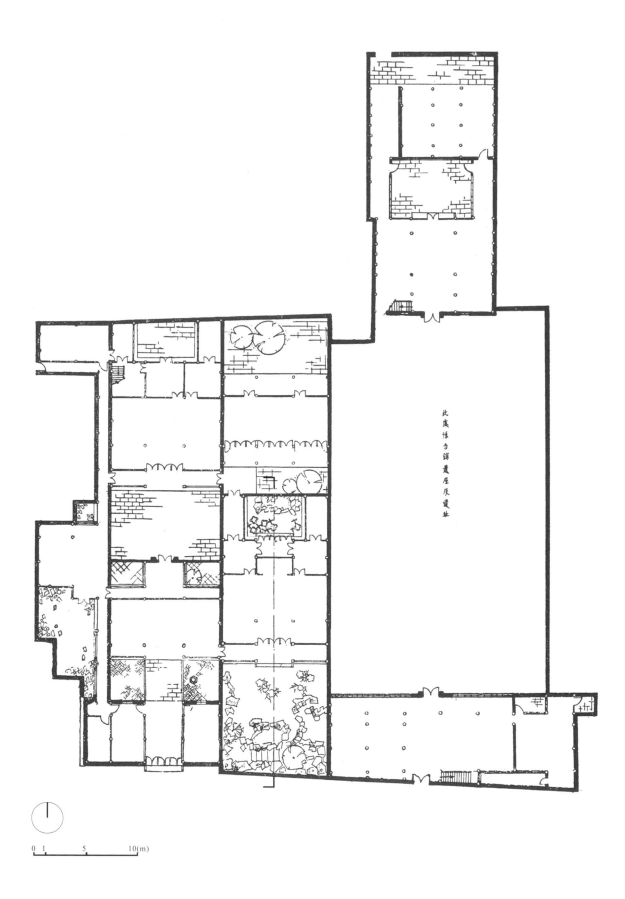

此廳係今錫麥屋反遺址

0 1　　5　　10(m)

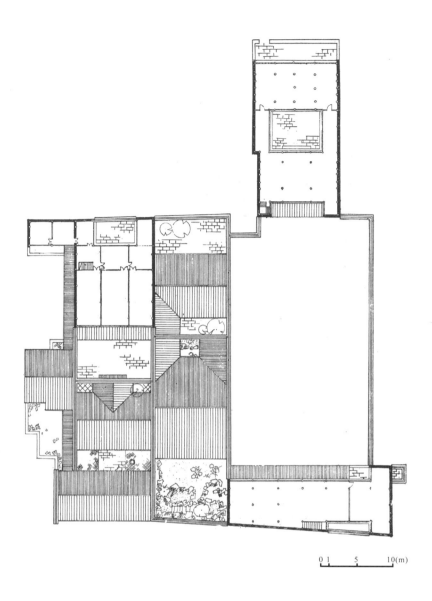

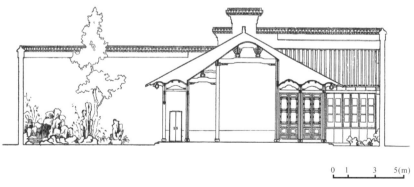

对页：修仙巷张宅一层平面图
本页上：修仙巷张宅二层平面图
本页下：修仙巷张宅花厅剖面图

Opposite: Ground floor plan of Zhang's residence at Xiuxian Alley
This page top: First floor plan of Zhang's residence at Xiuxian Alley
This page bottom: Section of flower hall of Zhang's residence at Xiuxian Alley

廖家巷刘宅　南向，东门，其平面为"H"形。楼厅三间，左右夹厢，前后各列两厢。厅前两侧者，东首为门屋，西首为书斋，其前则为一小天井。厅之西首隔避弄为一面阔三间楼厅，前辅以二厢。厅西书斋前后二间，为主人读书之处。此建筑虽由二组合成，但又可分别使用，宅东南两面设大门。厅后有"曰"形楼屋，天井小，通风、光线皆差，系红纸作坊，因当时主人经营此业。作坊旁为厨房及货房等地，更西有一小园。

Liu's residence at Liaojia Alley is a south facing residence with the entrance on the east side. It has an H-shaped floor plan. The two-story hall is three bays wide with two buildings on its side. There are two wings both in front of and behind the building. The east wing in front of the building is used as the gate house, and the west wing is used as the study. A small courtyard is in front of the hall. There is a three-bay-wide two-story building across the west end Bilong. This building has two wings in front. The front and rear of the west end study is where the owner reads. This residence is based on two groups of structures, but each can be used independently. There are gates to both the south and east side of the residence. There is another building behind the main hall. Its courtyard is rather small, and both air flow and lighting are extremely poor for this building. This is where red paper is manufactured. The owner at the time operated a business to produce red paper. The kitchen and storage warehouse are next to the workshop. There is a small garden further to the west.

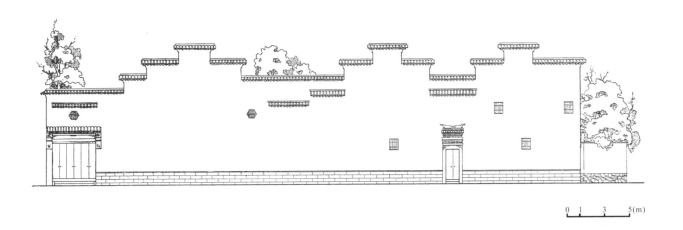

0 1   3   5(m)

0 1   3   5(m)

上：廖家巷刘宅东立面图
下：廖家巷刘宅剖面图

Top: East elevation of Liu's residence at Liaojia Alley
Bottom: Section of Liu's residence at Liaojia Alley

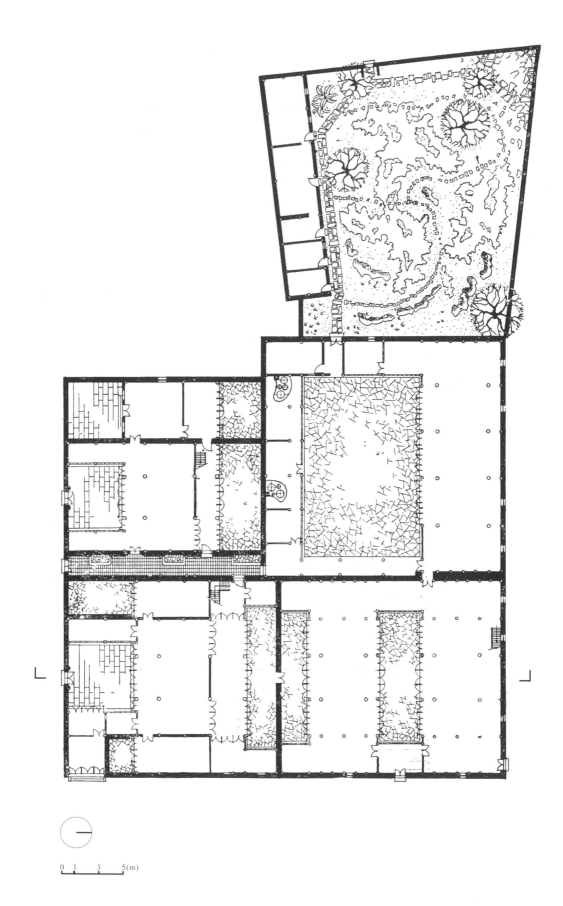

0 1   3   5(m)

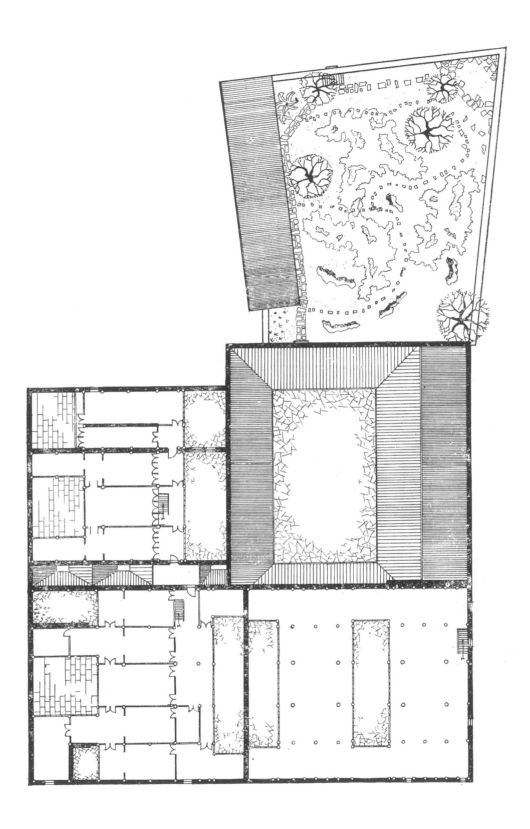

对页：廖家巷刘宅一层平面图
本页：廖家巷刘宅二层平面图

Opposite: Ground floor plan of Liu's residence at Liaojia Alley
This page: First floor plan of Liu's residence at Liaojia Alley

天官坊陆宅　是宅原为明代王鏊旧宅。王官至大学士，王芑孙《怡老园图记》所谓："当时先文恪公尚宝府君作居第城西，前曰柱国坊，后曰天官坊。又辟其余地为园，曰怡老园。入清朝以其第为江苏布政衙门，于是柱国天官之坊中断为二，子孙散处其间。今所居柱国坊，实当时园屋而已。"坊东名"学士街"，当时园西枕夏驾湖，临流筑室，城之雉堞映其前。今人称是湖及附近小流皆冠以王鏊之名，其源已是可知。宅于清乾隆壬子年（1792年）归陆义庵，现除正路部分尚存旧规外，东西则有所改建增筑。一宅之内包括住宅、祠堂、义庄及小型园林，其占地之广为苏州住宅之冠。

建筑物南向，中路以门屋、轿厅、大厅、女厅等为主。大厅面阔三间，进深特大，作纵长方形，前用翻轩（卷棚）；系明代所建，唯梁架入清已有部分修改。厅两侧分列书房，并兼作会客之用，平面狭长，前后间以小院。厅前门楼下原有戏台，今已毁，门楼

Lu's residence at Tianguan Fang belonged to Wang Ao during Ming dynasty. Wang has risen to the rank of Daxueshi. *The Map of Yilao Garden* (《怡老园图记》) by Wang Qisun said, "At that time Wenke (Wang Ao) chose the land at west side of the city to built his residence. The front portion was called Zhuguo Fang, and the back portion was named Tianguan Fang. The remaining land was used to construct a garden called Yilao Garden. The Buzheng office of Jiangsu province had used the front portion of this residence since Qing dynasty. The land had been broken into two halves. The family became scattered around the region. The residence at Zhuguo Fang was in fact the garden houses when this area was constructed." The road to the east of Tianguan Fang is called Xueshi Street. The garden lies next to Xiajia Lake, and buildings are located next to the waterscape. The city wall is reflected in the lake. The lake and small streams nearby are all named after Wang Ao. The reason is quite well known. The residence became the property of Lu Yi'an during Renzi year (1792) of Qianlong period of Qing dynasty. There are additions and changes made on the buildings in the east and west axis. The central axis still follows the old style. The residence includes residential area, family altar, residence for the poor, and a small garden. This residence occupies the largest land area among all Suzhou residences.

The south facing structures along the central axis include lobby, Jiaoting, main hall, and Nüting. The main hall has three bays and is especially deep with an elongated rectangle shape. There is a Fanxuan (翻轩 or Juanpeng 卷棚 , arched ceiling, which can be dedivided into multiple sections, each called one Juan) built in front of the building. The structure was built during Ming dynasty except some modifications of the frames during Qing dynasty. The two studies are located along both sides of the main hall. They are also used as an area for meeting guests. The floor plans for the two studies are narrow with front and rear gardens.

An opera platform in front of the main hall has been destroyed. The stone piece with exquisitely carved relief at the bottom of the gate tower was made during Ming dynasty. Nüting is five bays wide and two stories tall, with front and rear wings forming an H-shaped building. There is an seven-bay-wide two-story building behind Nüting used for family living. The Piwu is located behind for living space of servants in the house.

There is a hall on the east axis followed with ladies' living area, kitchen, and garden. The hall was built during Bingzi year (1816) of Jiaqing period during Qing dynasty. It is three bays wide and there were two wings on the side with the upper story used as an opera-viewing platform for the ladies. The east wing has been converted to a study. There is a flower hall to the east of the hall. The hillock is placed in front of the flower hall with another study around it. This is a later construction.

On the west axis are two small courtyards in addition to the flower hall, followed by three stages of masters' houses. Further to the rear, a covered bridge leads toward the back gate across the river.

The clerks' room is placed in several small houses at the start of the west axis. The family altar and residence for the poor is beyond the west axis. The family altar is very grand. The Pei family altar at Shizilin is based on this design. This design was also emulated by the Liu family of Nanxun in Wuxing area of Zhejiang province. It includes main gate, main hall, secondary hall, and two corridors along the side. The dining area to the east of the halls is where the whole family dine after sacrifice is made to the ancestors. There is a flower hall to the west of the altar. This is used to greet guests when sacrifice is presented to ancestors. There are hillocks placed in front of and behind the structure. The rice is dried on a field in front of the family altar.

底部之石刻犹是明代遗物，雕刻至精。女厅计楼五间，并缀厢楼，作"H"形平面，其后楼屋七间，亦作内眷居住之用。再后为披屋，系婢仆之居所。

东路有厅，后有居女眷之上房、厨房及花园。厅建于清嘉庆丙子年（1816年），面阔三间，东西山墙外紧贴厅屋者，原有两间夹厢，其上层为女宾观剧之处。今东首已改建为书房，不复旧观。厅东有花厅一，前置假山，绕以书斋，为新改建者。

西路除花厅外，其后杂以小院二，再后上房三进，最后为披屋，有暖桥（廊桥）过河，隔岸设后门。

账房置于大厅前，西首若干平屋。路外为家祠及义庄，此祠规模甚大，狮子林贝氏宗祠即仿此而建，浙江吴兴南浔刘氏者亦仿此。计分头门、大堂、二堂，旁翼两廊。堂东膳堂为祭祀时全族进餐之所。祠西为花厅，系祭祖时会宾之所，前后间列峰石。祠前为义庄晒谷场。

1. 旗杆 | Flagpole
2. 照壁 | Zhaobi
3. 大门 | Main gate
4. 门屋 | Lobby
5. 轿厅（茶厅）| Jiaoting (tea hall)
6. 戏台 (原建筑已毁）| Opera platfrom (destroyed)
7. 大厅（嘉寿堂）| Main hall (Jiashou Hall)
8. 女厅 | Nüting
9. 账房 | Clerk's room
10. 书房 | Study
11. 小家祠 | A small family altar
12. "上房" | Masters' house
13. "下房"（披屋）| Servants' room (Piwu)
14. 新厅（清荫堂）| New hall (Qingyin Hall)
15. 上有夹层系女宾观戏处 | With an upper story used
as an opera-viewing platform for the ladies
16. 小厨房 | Small kitchen
17. 原大厨房 | Original large kitchen
18. 已毁后园 | Destroyed rear garden
19. 粪池位置 | Septic tank
20. 水后门码头 | Rear gate by the river side as a pier
21. 花厅 | Flower hall
22. 河桥 | River bridge
23. 后门 | Rear gate
24. 后门门屋 |Lobby of rear gate
25. 膳堂 | Dining area
26. 祠堂晒谷场 | Drying field of family altar
27. 祠堂头门 | Main gate of family altar
28. 祠堂大堂 | Main hall of family altar
29. 祠堂二堂 | Secondary hall of family altar
30. 神位及寿材间 | Spirit tablet and coffin room
31. 贮藏室 | Storage
32. 西花厅 | West flower hall
33. 小花园 | Small garden
34. 园门 | Garden gate
35. 果木蔬菜园 | Garden of vegetables and fruits
36. 花园旧址 | Garden's former site
37. 女宾观戏处 | Opera-viewing platform for the ladies
38. 藏书楼 | Library

0 1   5   10(m)

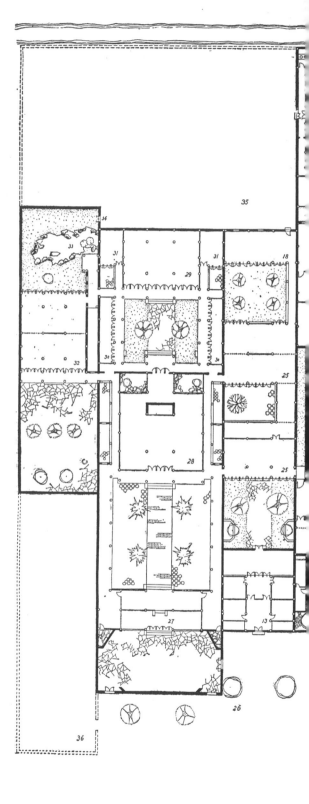

天官坊陆宅一层平面图

Ground floor plan of Lu's residence at Tianguan Fang

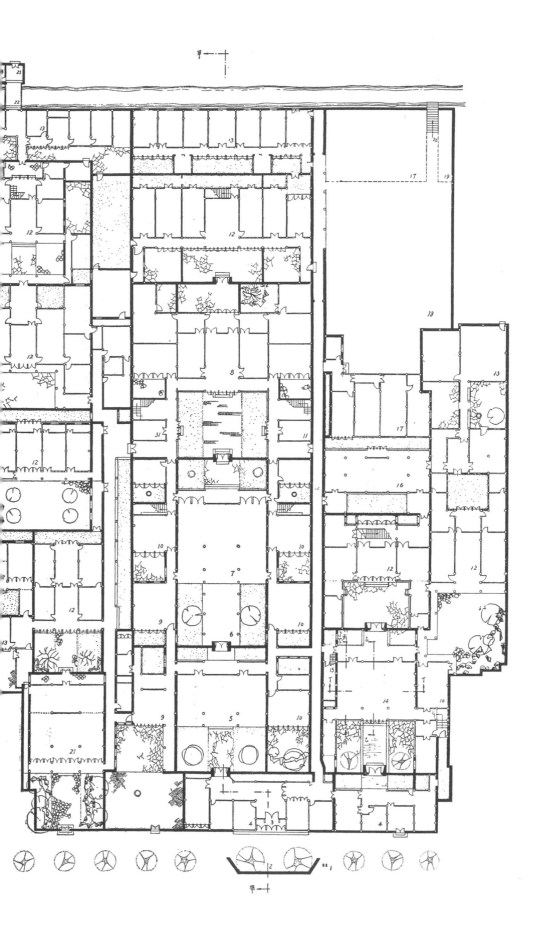

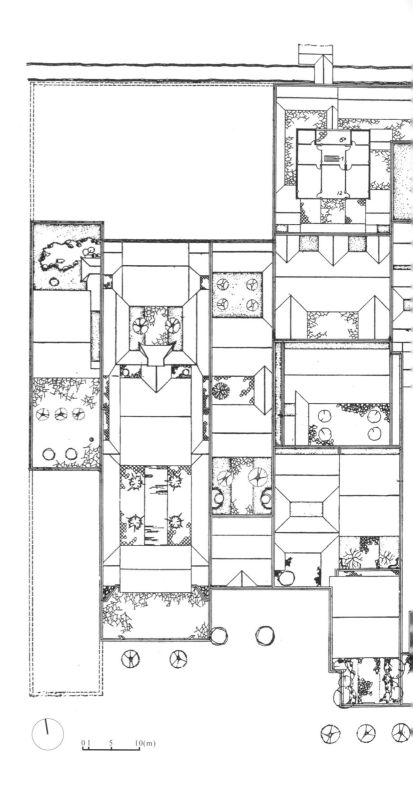

上：天官坊陆宅二层平面图
下：天官坊陆宅中轴线剖面图 甲—甲

0 1 3 5(m)

景德路杨宅 是宅明代为申时行宅，清乾隆时又属毕沅，至光绪年间为珠宝商杨洪源改建。宅南向略偏东，入门屋为轿厅、大厅。从大厅始包括其后各进，周以高垣，饰以华丽的砖刻门楼。大厅后女厅及上房三进，用两个三合院，中列一个四合院。四合院用走马楼（环楼），高畅宏大。最后的三合院亦用楼屋。东路前为账房，后为花厅二进，厅前各间列小院落，栽花垒石。再后为楼厅二，前者为曲尺形，后者为三合院。东西二路之间夹以长直避弄。平面极为规则，气魄宏大严谨。

西街曹宅 为学者曹元忠、元弼兄弟住宅，东向，正路为门屋、轿厅、大厅及女厅。而其北路诸屋皆南向，从避弄中入见次第列门。入其门皆有院落，或三间，或五间，并不在一直线上。院中植树栽花，各自成趣。此种布局不因朝向、地形而受限制，亦因地制宜之一法。大厅之南布置一狭长的花园，中凿池，前列花厅，西首有精舍数间，全园布局亦甚精巧。

Yang's residence on Jingde Road belonged to Shen Shixing during Ming dynasty. This residence belonged to Bi Yuan during Qianlong period of Qing dynasty. Jewelry shop owner Yang Hongyuan remodeled the residence during Guangxu period (1875–1908). The residence faces a south by east direction. The Jiaoting and main hall immediately follows the gate. The successive stages following the main hall are surrounded with high walls. The doorways between each stage have a very elaborately done brick carvings. Nüting, and three stages of masters' houses follow the main hall. The three masters' houses consist of one Siheyuan sandwiched by two Sanheyuan-type structures. The Siheyuan uses a Zoumalou style, which connects all four buildings together. This structure is especially grand. The Sanheyuan structure in the last stage is also a two-story building. The east axis starts with the clerks' room followed by two stages of flower halls. There are small gardens in front of each bay of flower hall. Flowers and hillocks are laid out accordingly. Two storied buildings are at the end of the residence. The front one is L-shaped and the back one is a Sanheyuan. There is a single long Bilong between the east and west axis. The floor plan is extremely structured. The residence is grand and rigorous.

Cao's residence on West Street is occupied by scholars and brothers Cao Yuanzhong and Cao Yuanbi. This residence faces to the east. The center axis consists of gate house, Jiaoting, main hall, and Nüting. The buildings along the north axis all face south, with doors of each courtyard facing Bilong. There is a garden for each building, and the buildings are three or five bays wide. These buildings along the north axis do not conform to a central axis. Trees and flowers are planted uniquely for each yard. This layout, which is another means of designing according to the land, does not conform to the constraints due to facing direction and lot shape There is a narrow and long garden on the south of the main hall. A pond is carved out in the middle of garden with a flower hall in front. Several small houses are located to the west end of the garden. The planning of the garden is especially exquisite.

Pan's residence on Nanshizi Street is an expansion done on the original residence by Pan Zuyin. This residence faces to the south, and is relatively recent among all the large residences in Suzhou. The construction of the residence occurred during Guangxu period of Qing dynasty. The houses purchased in various stages for the expansion had a few modifications made on them. There is a new central axis toward the east, and two-story structures were used for all the buildings. This is a very special case among the large residences found in Suzhou. The central axis can be divided into two sections that are surrounded by high walls. The front section uses a Siheyuan, and the back section uses a Sanheyuan together with a Siheyuan plan. There is no wall separating the front and back sections, which is very poised. The back section uses very large windows with open courtyards, making people feel clean and bright. The upper story of the corridors of Sanheyuan is where the ladies seat for watching operas. The railings are two-layered, which are extremely luxurious. The study to the east is L-shaped, and the garden can be reached on the south. The garden has a flower hall named Cizhenge. This is a three-bay-wide two-story building. The upper story floor is covered with square bricks. This structure has the most exquisite decorations in the residence. There is a three-bay family altar at the end of the east axis.

南石子街潘宅 为潘祖荫扩建，南向。是宅在苏州诸大宅中较为晚期，时间在清光绪年间。因此，除在原有分期购入的房屋基础上不加大变动外，在其东另建中路，各进皆用楼屋，为苏州大型住宅中之特例。中路可分前后二区，各周以高垣，前者用两个四合院，后者以一三合院与一四合院相套。前后二区之间皆无高墙作间隔，颇为落落大方，尤其后区户窗敞朗，天井广阔，予人以明爽的感觉。三合院两廊之楼为女宾观剧处，栏杆用两层，极尽豪华。东面书斋为曲尺形，向南可达花园。园尽头有花厅，名"赐珍阁"；三间，亦用楼屋，楼层铺整方砖，所用装修为此宅最精细。东路尽头有家祠三间。

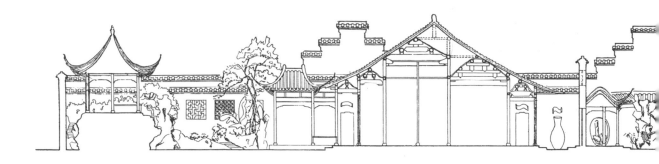

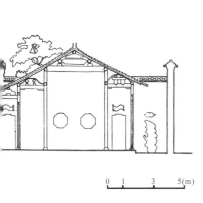

0 1   3   5(m)

0 1   5   10(m)

上：景德路杨宅花厅剖面图
对页下：景德路杨宅小院
本页：景德路杨宅一层平面图

Top: Section of flower hall of Yang's residence on Jingde Road
Opposite bottom: A small garden of Yang's residence on Jingde Road
This page: Ground floor plan of Yang's residence on Jingde Road

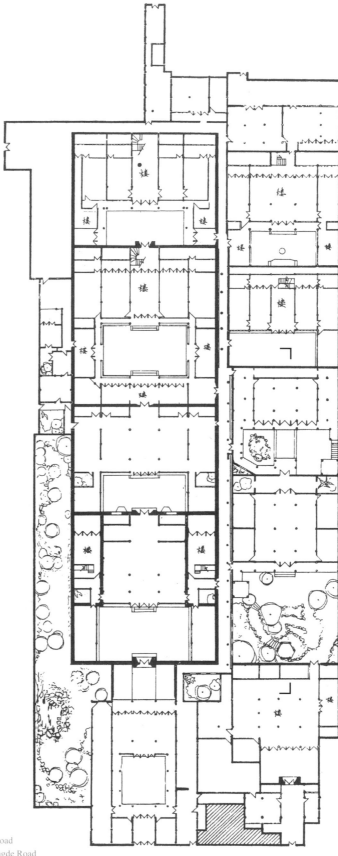

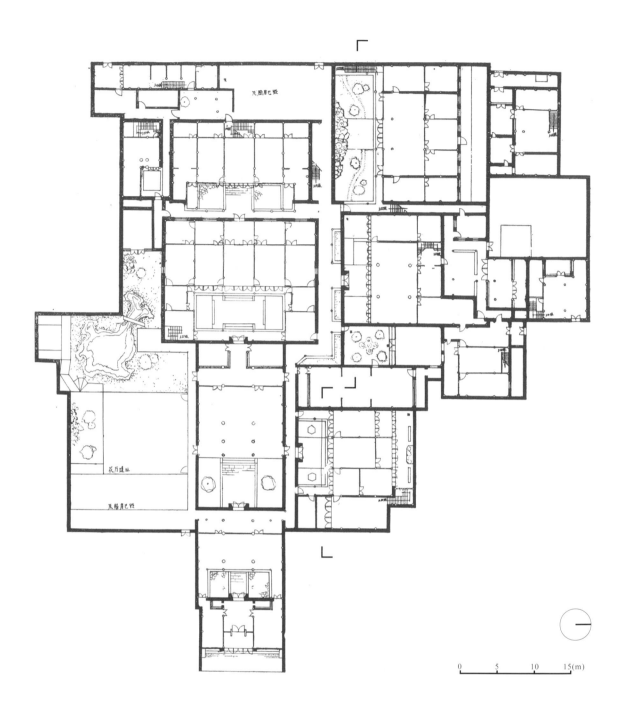

本页：西街曹宅一层平面图
对页上：西街曹宅二层平面图
对页下：西街曹宅北路剖面图

This page: Ground floor plan of Cao's residence on West Street
Opposite top: First floor plan of Cao's residence on West Street
Opposite bottom: Section along the north axis of Cao's residence on West Street

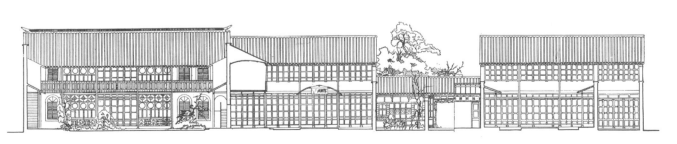

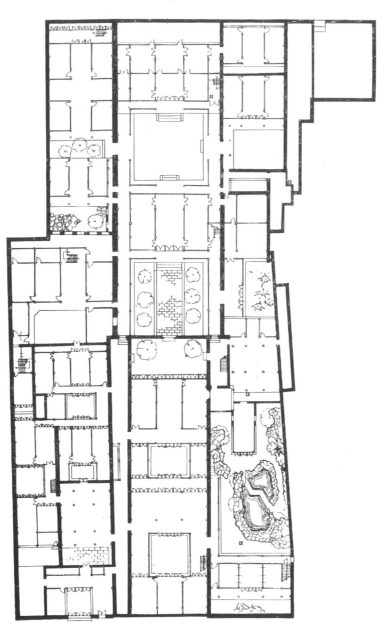

0 1　　5　　10(m)

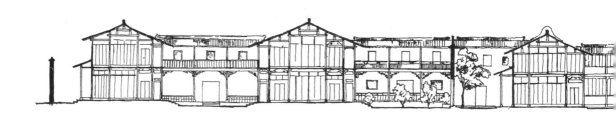

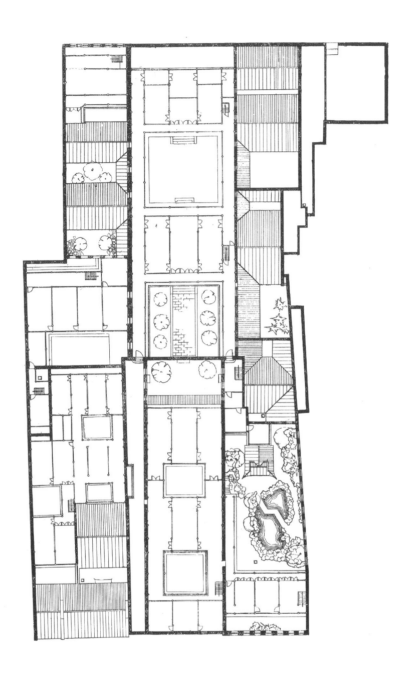

0 1   5   10(m)

对页上：南石子街潘宅一层平面图
本页上：南石子街潘宅二层平面图
下：南石子街潘宅剖面图

Opposite top: Ground floor plan of Pan's residence on Nanshizi Street
This page top: First floor plan of Pan's residence on Nanshizi Street
Bottom: Section of Pan's residence on Nanshizi Street

上：南石子街潘宅书房
下：南石子街潘宅楼厅

Top: Study of Pan's residence on Nanshizi Street
Bottom: Storied hall of Pan's residence on Nanshizi Street

南石子街潘宅装折

Decoration of Pan's residence on Nanshizi Street

铁瓶巷顾文彬宅　系就春申君祠扩建，除住宅外，隔巷尚有家祠、义庄，以及花园名"怡园"者，其营造年代为清同治末、光绪初。宅东南向，门前有照壁，照壁后为马厩、夫役室及河埠。大门内为轿厅，建于明末，用木栌。梁架为小五架梁，正如《园冶》所示者。旁为账房，入内为大厅，平面系纵长方形，建于清乾隆八年（1743年），厅前原有戏台今已毁，其左为书斋，有楼，楼上可为女宾观剧处。大厅后自成一区，由一三合院与一四合院相套，皆为女厅（上房），俱有楼。东路为花厅（名"艮庵"）与藏书楼（过云楼）组成一个四合院。花厅前

The residence of Gu Wenbin at Tieping Alley expands upon the temple of Chunshen Jun (春申君). There are a family altar, residence for the poor, and a garden called Yiyuan located across the road. The construction of this residence started around late Tongzhi (1862–1874) to early Guangxu period of Qing dynasty. The residence faces southeast with a Zhaobi in front of the gate. A stable, a servants' room, and a wharf are located behind the Zhaobi. A late Ming dynasty Jiaoting, the columns of which stand on wooden plinths, is located behind the main gate. The frame uses a miniature five-purlin-beam system exactly like those shown in *Yuanye*. The clerks' room is to the side, and the main hall is the next structure on the central axis. The main hall is an elongated rectangle shaped structure built during the eighth year (1743) of Qianlong period of Qing dynasty. The opera platform in front of the hall has been destroyed. The study is located to the left and the upper story is used as an opera viewing platform for the ladies. The structures behind main hall form an independent section. A Sanheyuan and a Siheyuan connect to each other. These two structures are both Nüting (masters' houses) that are two stories high. There is a flower hall named Gen'an on the east axis. This structure and the library building named Guoyunlou form a Siheyuan layout. There are hillocks placed in front of and behind the flower hall. The front hillock is especially grand. This large and elegant hillock, along with the Lingbi stone (located in Wangshi Garden currently) in Gen'an are extremely precious pieces. The structures are extremely luxurious and detailed with partitions made from gingko wood. There are two Sanheyuan located behind this section. This is where Gu Wenbin rested and lived. The bedrooms are all installed with floor screens, which use the best wood with fine carvings. The rest of the area in the east axis is separated into several small courtyards. There is one hall and two buildings that are two stories to form a Sanheyuan in the west axis. Small courtyards are also built in small parcels of land. The secret room in the hall is covered with a fake door to hide the existence of the room. This style is commonly seen in Suzhou residences. Peng's residence of Shijia Alley has two sets of secret rooms making it extremely secretive.

后皆列假山峰石，而厅前者尤具丘壑，其峰石之硕大、玲珑，与艮庵内之灵璧石（石今存网师园）皆为吴中珍品。建筑物极华丽精细，槅扇俱用银杏木。此区之后计前后两个三合院，为当时顾文彬退养起居的地方。卧室皆置地屏，装修用材、雕刻均为上选。再东除厅事外，其余皆就地形划为各小院。西路有厅一、楼二，为三合院，亦于隙地建小院。而厅旁密室掩于假门，不知其内尚有别居。此种手法在苏州住宅中惯用，如史家巷彭宅多至密室两重，曲房深户，令人莫测。

尚　　書　　里

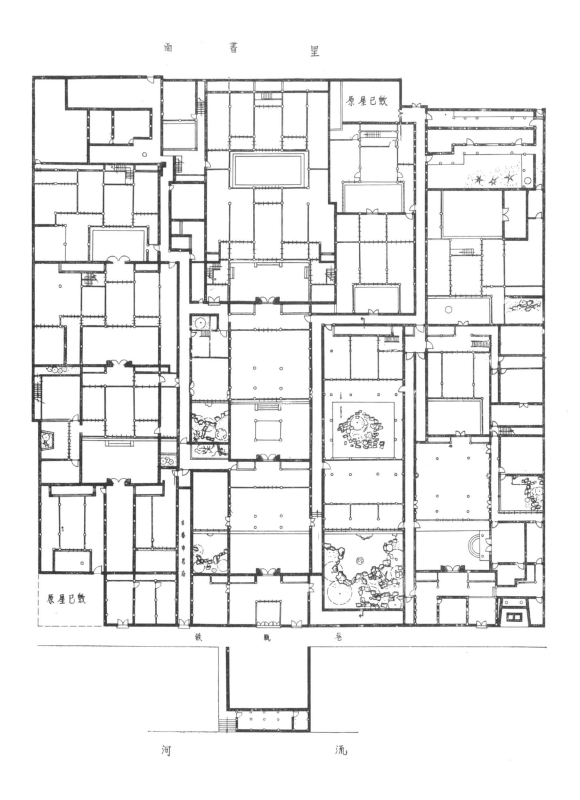

原屋已致

原屋已致

古春申君庙

原屋已致

铁　　瓶　　巷

河　　　　流

0 1　　5　　10(m)

54

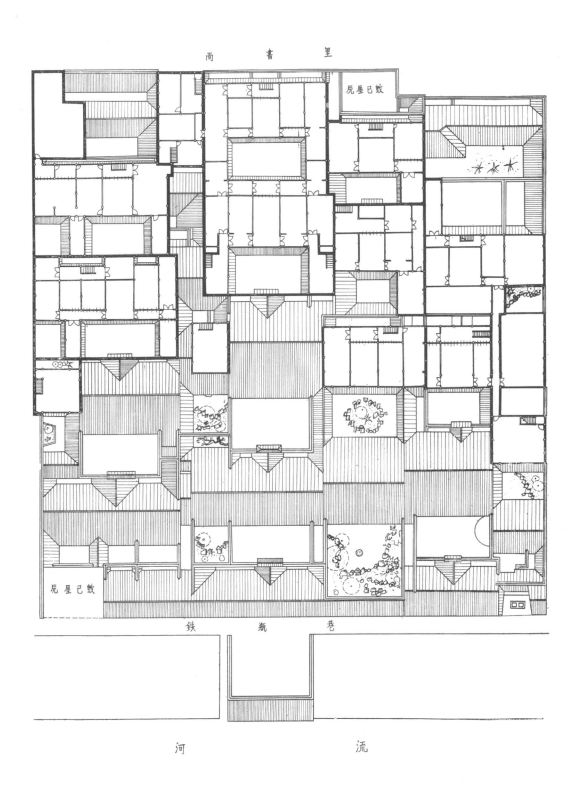

尚　書　里

厉屋已敚

厉屋已敚

铁　瓶　巷

河　　　流

对页：铁瓶巷顾宅一层平面图
本页：铁瓶巷顾宅二层平面图

Opposite: Ground floor plan of Gu's residence at Tieping Alley
This page: First floor plan of Gu's residence at Tieping Alley

上：东北街拙政园三十六鸳鸯馆内陈设
下：铁瓶巷顾宅花厅剖面图

Top: Furnishings at Thirty-Six Pairs of Mandarin Ducks Hall of
    Zhuozheng Garden
Bottom: Section of flower hall of Gu's residence at Tieping Alley

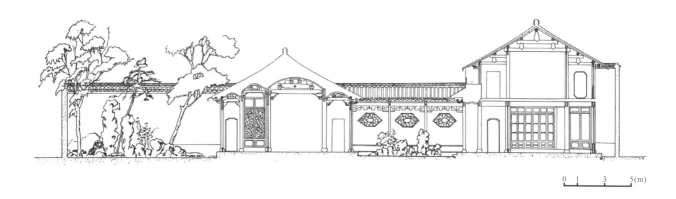

0 1 3   5(m)

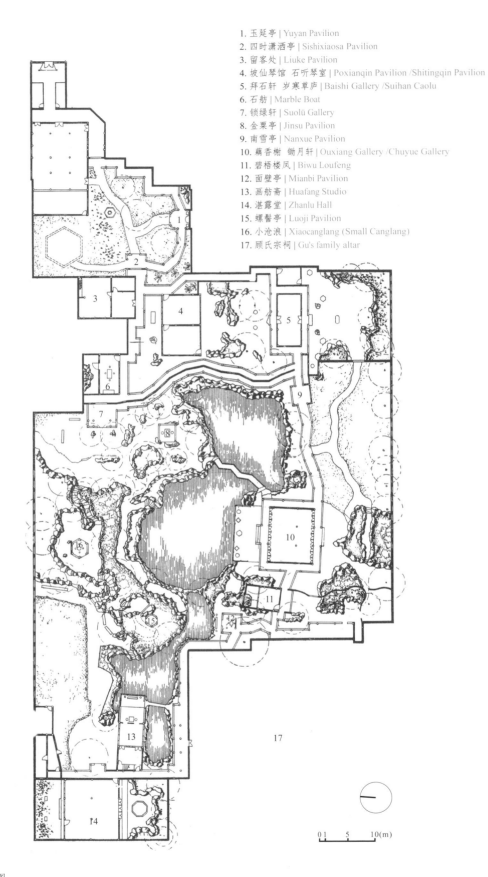

1. 玉延亭 | Yuyan Pavilion
2. 四时潇洒亭 | Sishixiaosa Pavilion
3. 留客处 | Liuke Pavilion
4. 坡仙琴馆 石听琴室 | Poxianqin Pavilion /Shitingqin Pavilion
5. 拜石轩 岁寒草庐 | Baishi Gallery /Suihan Caolu
6. 石舫 | Marble Boat
7. 锁绿轩 | Suolü Gallery
8. 金粟亭 | Jinsu Pavilion
9. 南雪亭 | Nanxue Pavilion
10. 藕香榭 锄月轩 | Ouxiang Gallery /Chuyue Gallery
11. 碧梧楼凤 | Biwu Loufeng
12. 面壁亭 | Mianbi Pavilion
13. 画舫斋 | Huafang Studio
14. 湛露堂 | Zhanlu Hall
15. 螺髻亭 | Luoji Pavilion
16. 小沧浪 | Xiaocanglang (Small Canglang)
17. 顾氏宗祠 | Gu's family altar

0 1   5   10(m)

怡园一层平面图

Ground floor plan of Yiyuan Garden

铁瓶巷任宅 清同治、光绪年间任道熔建，东南向，门前原有大照壁及东西辕门，其气魄之大为苏州住宅之冠，惜已毁。中路为门屋、轿厅，构成四合院。入内为大厅，其后女厅（上房）二进，翼前后厢，构成"H"形平面，而厅旁二厢与厅不相联。中间小院，其于梢间采光与通风均多好处。东路为花厅，厅南建一小型戏台，台东有二亭，皆沿墙以廊缀之，而花木皆不植在中线上，通畅视线。厅东书房建有楼，可作女宾观剧之用。厅西有船轩一，其后有小院一二处，颇为空灵曲折。花厅后尚有楼厅二，皆三合院楼，自成一区，系上房。西花厅为前后对照式，东面用廊联之，厅前皆置山石花木。住宅其余隙地则按地形安排小院落。是宅特征在花厅数量增多，建筑精细。戏台不置大厅前而移至花厅部分，宅内绿化面积增多，装修益踵事增华，其挺秀明快处，在原有形式上有所进展。

Ren's residence at Tieping Alley was built by Ren Daorong between late Tongzhi and early Guangxu periods of Qing dynasty. The building faces to the southeast, and there was a large Zhaobi with both east and west Yuanmen outside the main gate. This was the most impressive among all the residences in Suzhou, but was unfortunately destroyed. The central axis consist of a Siheyuan formed by Jiaoting and gate house. The main gate follows with two stages of Nüting (masters' house). There are wings to the front and back of the masters' house to form an H-shaped floor plan. The wings are not connected to the hall. There is a small garden in the middle. This is very advantageous in improving the lighting and ventilation of end bays. There is a flower hall on the east axis. A small opera platform is built toward the south of the hall. The two pavilions to the east of the platform are built along the wall and connected by corridors. No flowers or trees are planted along a central axis. This opens up the view on the central axis. The study to the east of the hall is a two-story building. The upper story might be used for ladies to watch the opera. There is a ship-shaped Xuan to the west of the hall with several small courtyards behind it. This is a scene that can hardly be penned in a couple of lines. There are two Sanheyuan with multi-story halls behind the flower hall, which form an indepedent section to be masters' houses. The west flower hall has front and rear sections and the east side has a corridor connection. In the courtyard in front of the hall, hillocks, trees and flowers are placed. Small courtyards designed to fit the various shape of remaining open space are spread across the lot. The residence is characterized by increased number of flower halls and detailed buildings. The opera platfrom is moved from the main hall to the flower hall section There is a significant increase in green space. The decorations improved from original style to be more elaborate and elegant, and brighter as well.

Liu's residence at Xiaoxinqiao Alley is also known as Ouyuan Garden (the Couple's Garden Retreat). Lu Jin built this residence during early Qing dynasty. It then became the summer house of the Zhu family. Shen Bingcheng became the owner of this residence since Tongzhi period of Qing dynasty. This residence is surrounded by river on east, south and north sides. The main gate is on the south side. The central section is formed by four stages of structures. The central axis starts with gate house, followed by Jiaoting, main hall, and trailed by Nüting. The gate house and Jiaoting both use a wide rectangle floor plan. An elongated rectangle floor plan is used to design the main hall. The Nüting at the fourth stage is five bays wide and forms its own section. Two opposing units of Sanheyuan form an H-shaped floor plan in this section. No Bilong is built alongside the central axis. Two small units of Siheyuan are at both sides of the last stage. The placement of L-shaped structure and Sanheyuan in front of these smaller courtyards presents some quite thoughtful styles. The other sections like the connection from the east and west garden to the main residence, and the combination of houses with the style of garden are all done to the point. The east garden is where the owner relaxes. The small flower hall coupled with a multi-level winding passage connects to the two-story building at the northeast corner. There is a very scenic hillock placed in front of the building. The west garden is a studying place for the owner. There are many plants and hillocks placed beside the building. A small veranda on the east side connects to a sloping corridor towards the southwest leading to the private school in the front. There is a L-shaped building served as a library hidden beyond the hillocks behind the study. The garden Ouyuan is famous for its buildings. It is very unique among all the gardens in the Suzhou area.

小新桥巷刘宅 即耦园。为清初陆锦所建，继为祝氏别业，同治后属沈秉成。此宅东、南、北三面绕河，大门设于南面，中央部分由门屋、轿厅、大厅、女厅等四进组成。门屋与轿厅皆用横长方形平面，大厅采纵长方形平面。到第四进女厅，面阔增至五间，自成一区，用两个相反的三合院构成"H"形平面。中轴旁未置避弄，而第四进的两侧各建小四合院，再在其前配以曲尺形与三合院等，自能独出心机。其他部分如东、西二花园与住宅的联系，以及房屋与园林疏密的配合，皆能恰到好处。东园为主人燕游之处，自小花厅起，以高低曲廊通至东北角的重楼，楼前山石峥嵘。西园为主人读书处，前后罗列山石花木，又自东侧小轩斜廊西南行，通至前部书塾。书斋后部隔山石建有曲尺形藏书楼，极曲折之致。耦园以楼胜，为吴中园林别树一格。

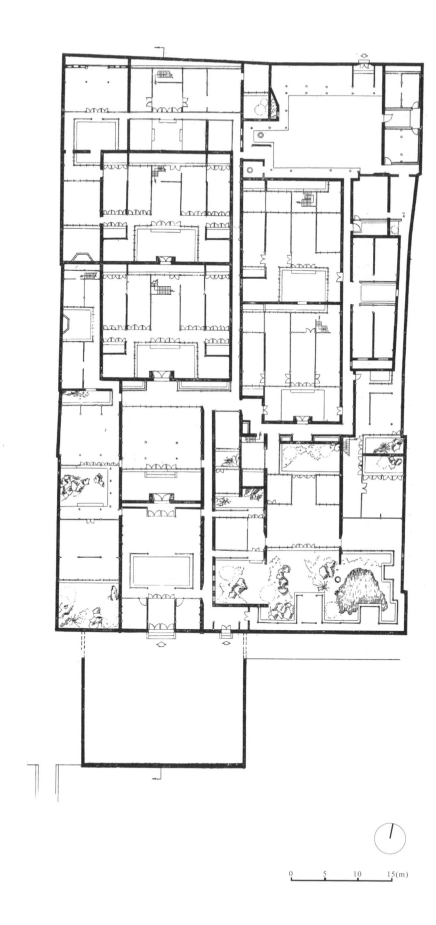

0   5   10   15(m)

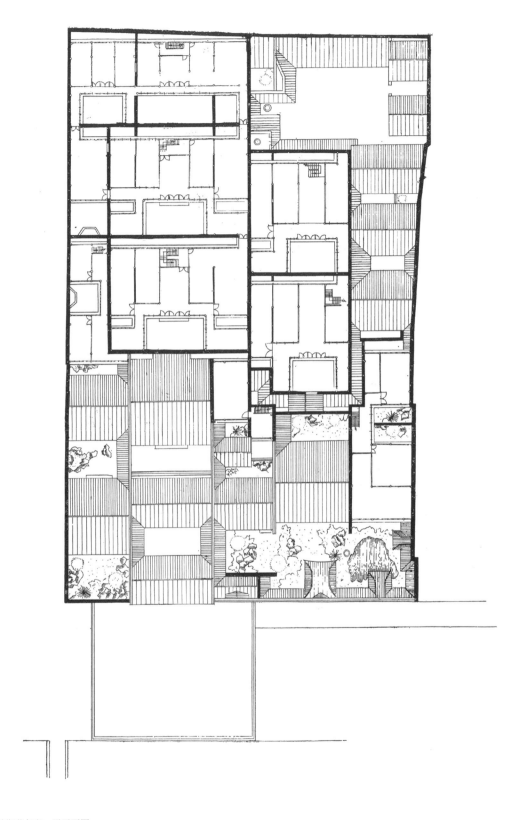

对页：铁瓶巷任宅一层平面图
本页：铁瓶巷任宅二层平面图

Opposite: Ground floor plan of Ren's residence at Tieping Alley
This page: First floor plan of Ren's residence at Tieping Alley

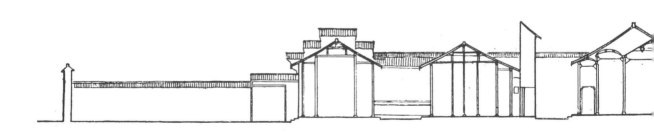

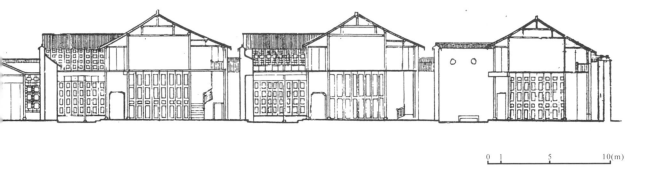

对页上：铁瓶巷任宅山墙
本页上：铁瓶巷任宅门楼
 下：铁瓶巷任宅剖面图

Opposite top: Gable end of Ren's residence at Tieping Alley
This page top: Gate tower of Ren's residence at Tieping Alley
Bottom: Section of Ren's residence at Tieping Alley

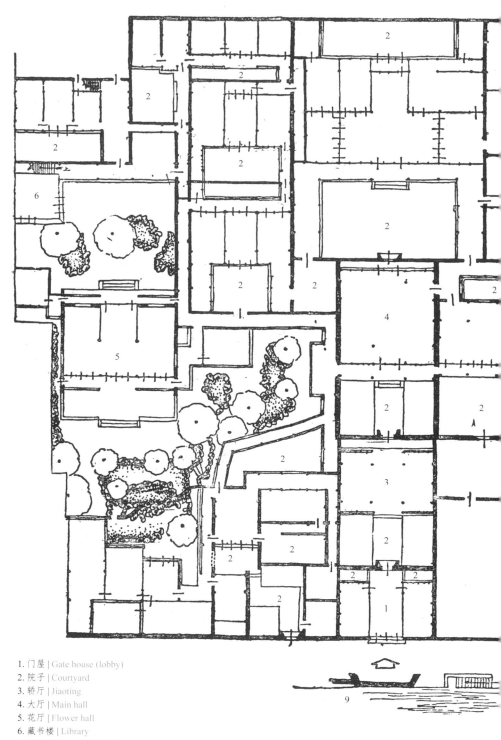

1. 门屋 | Gate house (lobby)
2. 院子 | Courtyard
3. 轿厅 | Jiaoting
4. 大厅 | Main hall
5. 花厅 | Flower hall
6. 藏书楼 | Library
7. 四面厅 | Four-Sided hall
8. 亭 | Pavilion
9. 河 | River

0   2   10   20(m)

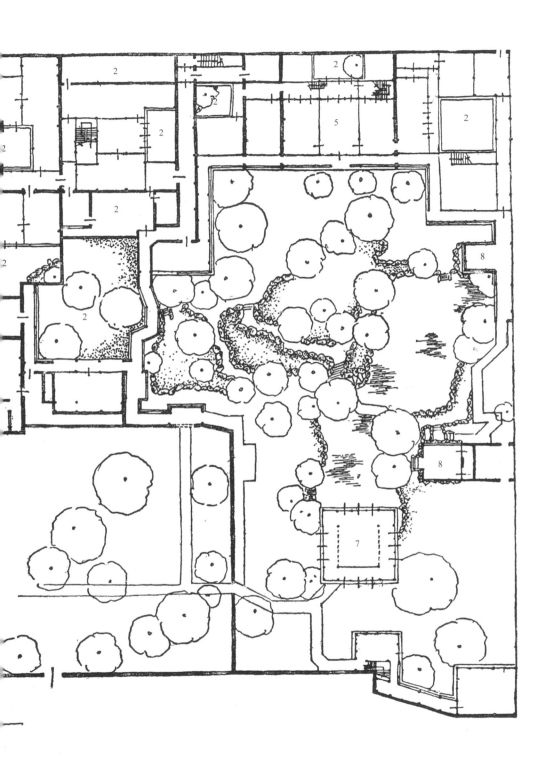

2
2
5
2
2
2
2
2
2
2
8
8
7

小新桥巷耦园刘宅一层平面图

Ground floor plan of Ouyuan Garden

苏州城东西长 3.1 千米，南北长 4.4 千米，是面积约为 14 平方千米的矩形城市。街坊面积为 13.4 平方千米，建筑占地面积为 11.3 平方千米，建筑密度为 38%。现有 60 多个街坊。每个街坊面积小的有 3.5 公顷，大的有 55.6 公顷，一般在 20 ～ 30 公顷间。城内道路纵横，道路系统亦与住宅相平行。从南宋理宗绍定二年（1229 年）所刻的《平江图》看，街坊情况与今日现状相对照变动甚微，若干坊名尚沿其旧。城内主要干道为南北向，如临顿路、人民路，东西干道如观前街、景德路、东中市、道前街等。坊巷则极多数东西向，可以通至干道。东西向的巷与巷间距一般在 80 ～ 120 米之间，巷的宽度最狭的在 1.5 米左右，巷长一般在 200 ～ 400 米之间。河流一般宽度为 2 ～ 3 米，最狭为 1.9 米。水坡 1/100 000，水位差仅为 2 ～ 4 厘米。住宅在城市中的总体布局有下列各种情况。

The city of Suzhou is 3.1 kilometers wide along the east and west direction, and 4.4 kilometers long on the north and south direction. It occupies a rectangular shaped area of approximately fourteen square kilometers. The city blocks occupy about 13.4 square kilometers of this total area. The building area is about 11.3 square kilometers, and building density is at about thirty-eight percent. There are over sixty city blocks that vary in size from 3.5 hectares to 55.6 hectares. The average size of a city block is between twenty to thirty hectares. The residences are situated parallel to the major roads. The roads and streets in the city have changed very little compared with those on the *Map of Pingjiang* drawn in 1229 (2nd year of Shaoding period during reign of Emperor Lizong of South Song dynasty). There are several city blocks that are still using the name used during South Song dynasty. The major roads along a north south direction like Lindun Road, Renmin Road. Guanqian Street, Jingde Road, Dongzhongshi, and Daoqian Steet are all major east west direction thoroughfares. The access lanes or alleys (Xiang) of blocks can reach major passages on both east and west ends. The distance between these east west direction lanes is typically between eighty and one hundred twenty meters. The narrowest of these passages can be at about only 1.5 meters wide. The passage way averages about two to four hundred meters long. Streams are about two to three meters wide, and the narrowest stream is only 1.9 meters wide. The water slope is at one in one hundred thousandth with only two to four centimeters of drop in elevation across the city. The distribution of residences across the city has the following eight characteristics.

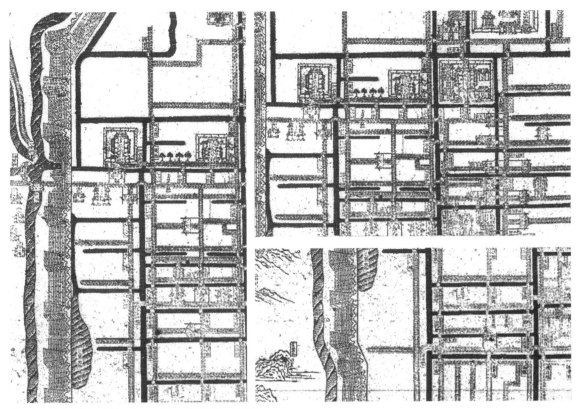

上：南宋赵昀（理宗）绍定二年（1229）《平江图》（局部）
下：盘门

Top: Part of the *Map of Pingjiang* drawn in 1229
Bottom: Gate Pan

带城桥沿河住宅

Residences by river at Daichengqiao

上：大儒巷沿河住宅
下：蒌葭巷沿河住宅

Top: Residences by river at Daru Alley
Bottom: Residences by river at Luxia Alley

白塔子桥沿河住宅

Residences by river at Baitaziqiao

上：张家巷沿河住宅
下：学士街沿河住宅

Top: Residences by river at Zhangjia Alley
Bottom: Residences by river on Xueshi Street

一、 城南城北住宅少。一方面，因过去每有兵乱，南北为入城主道，近城不安全，另一方面距市区也较远。

二、 主要市区在观前一带，因此大第宅皆在观前两端为多，其次为景德路、东中市两侧及阊门附近，以该处亦有商业市集。再城东北隅临顿路及城东南葑门附近亦有少数第宅。东城以居富商为多，西城以居官宦为多，所谓："坊，方也。以类聚居者，必求其类。"到清末，西城逐渐由新兴资本家代替旧居的官宦，而东城却渐增官宦住宅。

三、 坊巷与河流相平行，故巷有三种情况：其一，两巷沿河；其二，一巷沿河；其三，巷前后无河流。在前两种情况下，柴米等运输可由前门或后门入，但在后者情况下，是利用坊巷两头南北向河流。

四、 南北向的坊巷，建筑物有下列情况：甲、东西向；乙、东门南向；丙、西门南向；丁、西门北向等。这些住宅所处街坊大多是一面沿河，房

1. There are few residences located along the north and south part of the city. Because the north and south side are major entrances to the city and far from the downtown area, it may be unsafe to live there during war time.

2. The large residences are concentrated mostly along Guanqian Street, which is a major business thoroughfare. There are some small concentrations along Jingde Road, Dongzhonshi, and near Gate Chang which are all major business hubs of the city. In addition, there are residences on Lindun Road located at the southeast side, and Gate Feng at southeast side. The residents on the east side are mostly rich business owners, and most aristocrats take up residence on the west side. Such assembling inhabitation is reasonably described, "The Chinese word Fang (坊) means city square or block. People prefer to live and congregate near each other of the same or similar backgrounds, or professions. New residents will always live near others of similar experience or skill etc." The aristocrats residing in the west side of the city were gradually replaced by newly rising industrialists, and some more aristocrats have also taken residence in the east side in recent periods.

3. The access lane or alley (Xiang or 巷) in each block is parallel to streams or some waterways. So there are three types of lanes: first, lanes along both sides of the river; second, lanes only by one side of the river; third, no waterway running by the lanes. The daily necessities like rice can be transported into residences by means of waterways. In the first two scenarios goods can be directly transported to the front or rear of the building. The last scenario requires goods sent along north south direction waterway, and transported via land to the residences.

4. The buildings situated along north south direction access lanes are laid out in one of four fashions:

– Building facing west or east;

– Main gate located on east wall with building facing south;

– Main gate located on west wall with building facing south;

– Main gate located on west wall with building facing north.

These residences usually border stream on one side, and are located on very shallow plots of land. The direction faced by this type of building is not very desirable. The riches of the society do not occupy these houses. One can find this type of residence on the side of large residences, or along narrow and twisting access lanes. These buildings are often built and rented out by the landowners to craftsman, store clerks, and artisans residing in the city, as well as low and middle income residents. The buildings close to the streets usually have floor plans of H shape, Sanheyuan, L shape, or wide rectangular shape.

5. The residential compounds located on east west direction access lanes can all have south facing buildings. In order to maximize the availability of south facing residences, the building expands in depth, and has a very narrow front. This layout dictates the multi-staged, self-contained courtyard style to be used. There are instances where a great distance between two access lanes exists, and a single residence cannot occupy the whole area. In these cases some of the reverse sited plots are built with building facing away from the main gate to take advantage of south facing directions. This makes mixed north and south facing buildings a necessity in these residences. Those non-living areas face the north while the living areas face the south. As it is said in the Chapter of Residences of *Yijiayan*（《一家言》），"The right direction of a house is to face south, but this is not always attainable. In this case north facing buildings shall leave space and

屋进深很小，朝向又差，过去皆非富室大房所居。更有是在南北向大住宅之旁、曲巷滩地之间，由富室大户建造小型房屋，经营出租牟利，手工业者及普通中、小市民类多居之。平面为"H"形、三合院、曲尺形或横长方形的沿街建筑。

五、因为坊巷东西向，在这些坊巷中的建筑皆可南向，为了争取朝南的土地，遂形成纵向发展的建筑，利用逐进封闭性的院落式方式布局。至于有些两巷之间的距离过大，不可能为一宅所占用，若干住宅因此北向建造。在此种情况下为了得到朝南的朝向，形成了南北向混合的建筑群，如前数进非居住部分北向，其后居住部分则南向，即《一家言·居室部》所云："屋以面南为正向，然不可必得，则面北者宜虚其后，以受南薰。面东者虚右，面西者虚左，亦犹是也。"更有利用火弄（边弄）作通道，形成北基南向。

六、 在总体上，住宅厅堂一般皆为面阔三间，在大型住宅至女厅（上房）后部分，始有面阔五间以上者，不过从次间或稍间起必间隔，其原因是受当时制度的限制。按《明史·舆服志》："庶民庐舍，洪武二十六年定制不过三间五架，不许用斗拱饰彩色。三十五年复申禁饬，不许造九五间数房屋，虽至一二十所，随其物力，但不许过三间。正统十二年令稍变通之，庶民房屋架多而间少者不在禁限。"从今日苏州旧住宅来看，尚存此制。如天官坊陆宅，大厅面阔三间，而平面却为纵长方形，在架方面增加了。入清以后，清制虽无明代规定之严格，然在平面上还保存着部分明代的遗规，正如王芑孙《怡老园图记》上说："顺治、康熙间士大夫犹承故明遗习，崇治居室。"及证以今日所存清初第宅，其梗概可知。清代虽然在平面上限于面阔三间，但在厅旁次间墙外各加一间来变通，或用东西避弄将厅间数目在左右两翼增加，多者用避弄四条，朝横向大事扩展。因此大型住宅在平面上，大厅总以面阔三

open windows on the back for sunlight. Similarly east facing buildings shall open windows on the right hand side, and west facing buildings shall open windows on left hand side for the same reason." It is also possible to utilize fire access lanes also known as side lanes or Bianlong (边弄) in Chinese as main passage. This opens the possibility to build south facing houses on a north facing lot.

6. In general the halls of a compound are three bays wide, and they may increase to five or more bays wide starting from Nüting section of a large residence. There is always some form of separation at either the Cijian or Shaojian (the bays beside the three main bays) section of a hall due to regulations stipulated at that time. The chapter Yufuzhi in *Mingshi* (《明史》) stated, "During the 26th year of Hongwu period the building regulations for civilian residences limit the width to three bays wide, and no more than five purlins deep. The support braces (Dougong) cannot be used, and the structure cannot be painted with color. This rule was reemphasized during the 35th year of Hongwu period. It was also stipulated that number of purlins and bays may not be in multiples of nine and five. Although the total number of buildings can reach over twenty based on affordability, but a building cannot exceed three bays wide. This rule was slightly adjusted during the 12th year of Zhengtong period that a narrow building with many purlins can be exempted from the rule." The effect of this rule is very evident on many of the existing residences in Suzhou today. Lu's residence at Tianguan Fang has a main hall that is three bays wide, and the floor plan reflects an elongated rectangular shape with increased depth. The building regulation of Qing dynasty was not so strict, but many of the old rules were inherited. Wang Qisun stated in *The Map of Yilao Garden* (《怡老园图记》)that during the periods of Emperor Shunzhi (1644–1661) and Kangxi (1662–1722) the aristocrats still followed

Ming traditions in house design. This can be further illustrated in existing early Qing dynasty residences. The restriction of three bays width still applies to many of the buildings in Qing dynasty, but there could be implementations. An additional room adjacent to exterior wall or Bilong can add more rooms on both sides. There are some cases that as many as four Bilong are used to expand houses in width. The large residences typically maintain three-bay main halls. A study or a small Huating (flower hall) is located on small plots by the side. The width starting at the Nüting stage would increase to five bays wide. Zhang's residence at Kuojietou Alley (also known as Wangshi Garden) has a lot that widens toward the back. This makes it possible to construct a Nüting that is six bays wide. There exist low walls to divide the courtyard making the building appear five bays wide on the exterior. The living areas of Wu's residence at Fanmenqiao Long and Lu's residence at Tianguan Fang all reach seven bays wide. In general halls located on the central axis toward the rear of a residence are much wider than those in the front.

7. The landscaping is an integral part of Suzhou residences. Large gardens cover a large area beside the residence, moreover, rocks from Taihu Lake, flowers, trees, pavilions, or winding paths can be found in these residences. The small but exquisite gardens are built on small parcels of land like Quyuan Garden of Yu's residence at Mayike Alley, Wu's residence at Zhuangjiaqiao Alley. The ratio of green space to building area increased over time. This also holds true for courtyard spaces.

8. There are small alleys perpendicular to the access lanes. These lanes facilitate the transportaion between two long parallel access lanes. There are also many single ended private alleys. These alleys lead to the side door of a residence.

间为主，旁以隙地建书房或小花厅等，至女厅后开始面阔增多，一般以五间为习。阔街头巷张宅（网师园），因基地向后渐大，故其女厅面阔六间，天井两侧以短垣分隔，故外表仍为五间。而梵门桥弄吴宅及天官坊陆宅等后进上房，面阔皆多至七间。在总体看来，中轴线上是后部厅堂总的面阔大于前部厅堂了。

七、苏州住宅能将房屋与绿化地带有机地联系。除大型园林在住宅旁占地很广外，普通住宅在院子中皆略置湖石、栽花树，或间列亭阁，绕以回廊等。至于利用隙地，或长或曲，随宜布置得皆为极好的园林小品，如马医科巷俞宅曲园，装驾桥巷吴宅等。至于绿地面积与建筑物的比例，时期愈后绿地面积尽可能范围增大，天井的大小亦同样情形。

八、坊巷中还有小弄，为两巷的中部联系，俾使居民到邻巷不必绕道而行。更有许多私弄，只一面可通，引深到巷的腹部，以利侧门的通行。

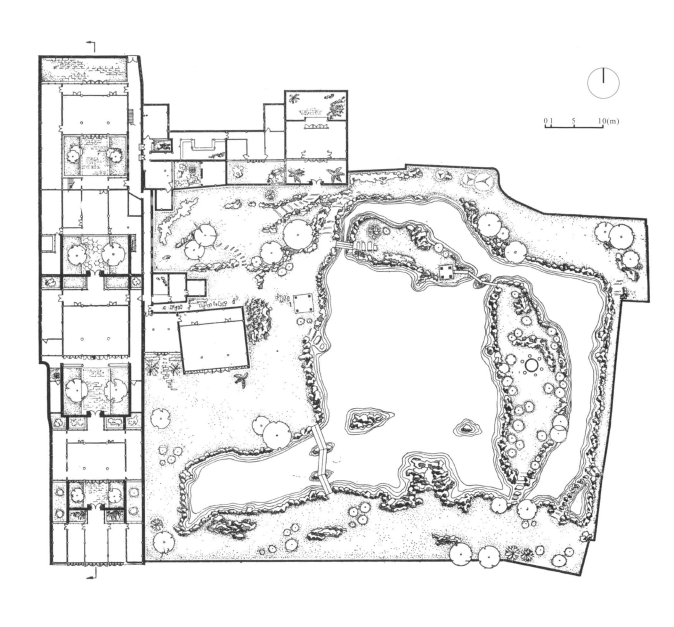

本页上：景德路毕宅一层平面图
对页上：景德路毕宅二层平面图
下：景德路毕宅剖面图

Opposite top: Ground floor plan of Bi's residence on Jingde Road
This page top: First floor plan of Bi's residence on Jingde Road
Bottom: Section of Bi's residence on Jingde Road

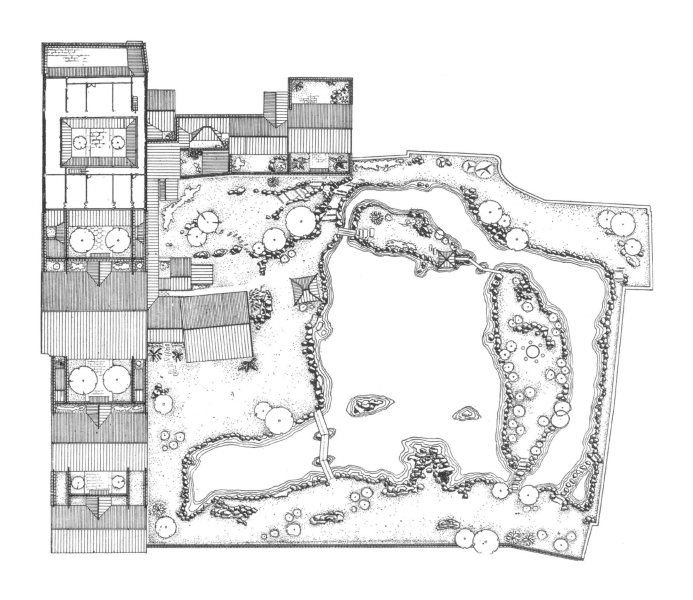

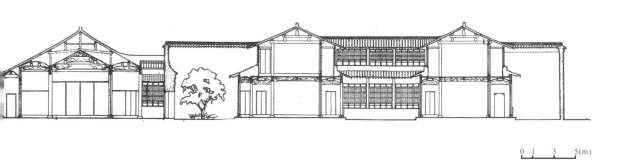

0 1   3   5(m)

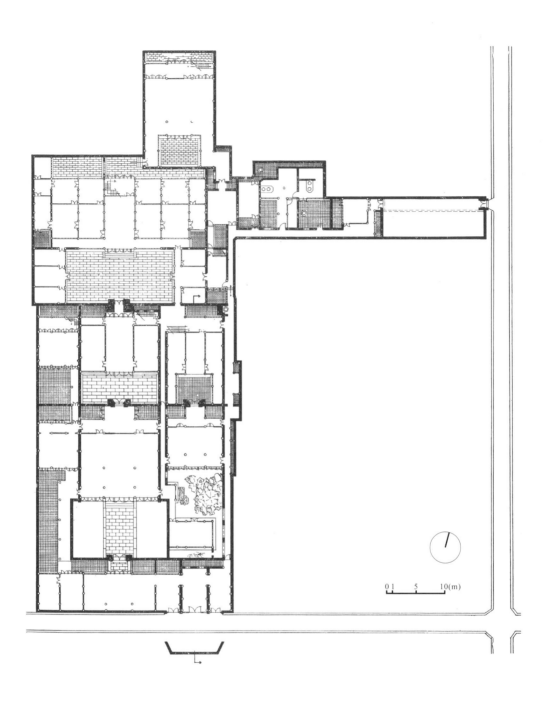

本页上：梵门桥弄吴宅一层平面图
对页上：梵门桥弄吴宅二层平面图
下：梵门桥弄吴宅花园剖面图

This page top: Ground floor plan of Wu's residence at Fanmenqiao Long
Opposite top: First floor plan of Wu's residence at Fanmenqiao Long
Bottom: Section of garden of Wu's residence at Fanmenqiao Long

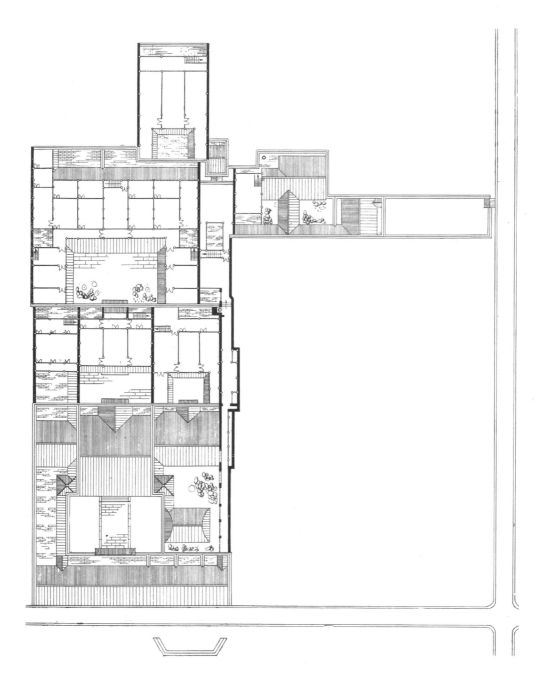

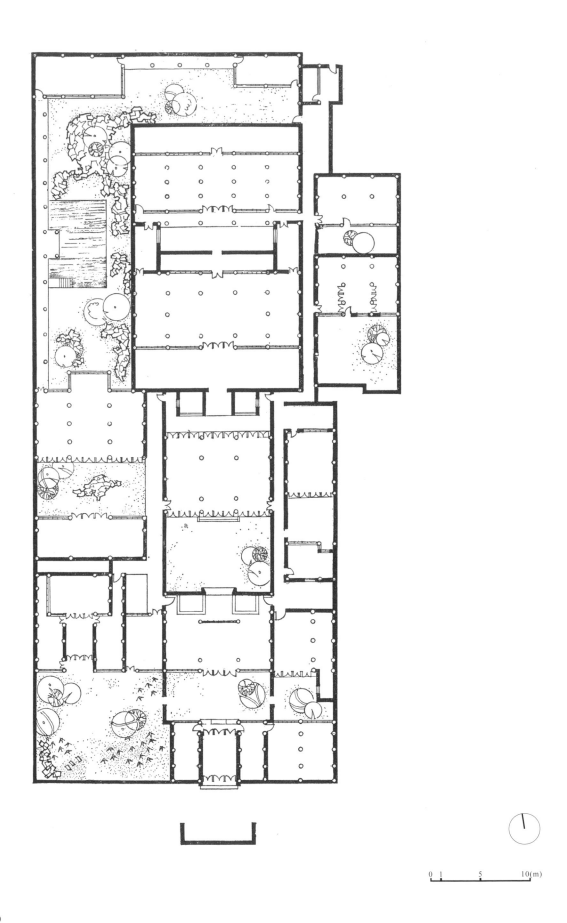

0 1 5 10(m)

对页：马医科巷俞宅曲园一层平面图
本页：韩家巷鹤园曲廊

Opposite: Ground floor plan of Quyuan Garden
This page: Winding corridor of Crane Garden

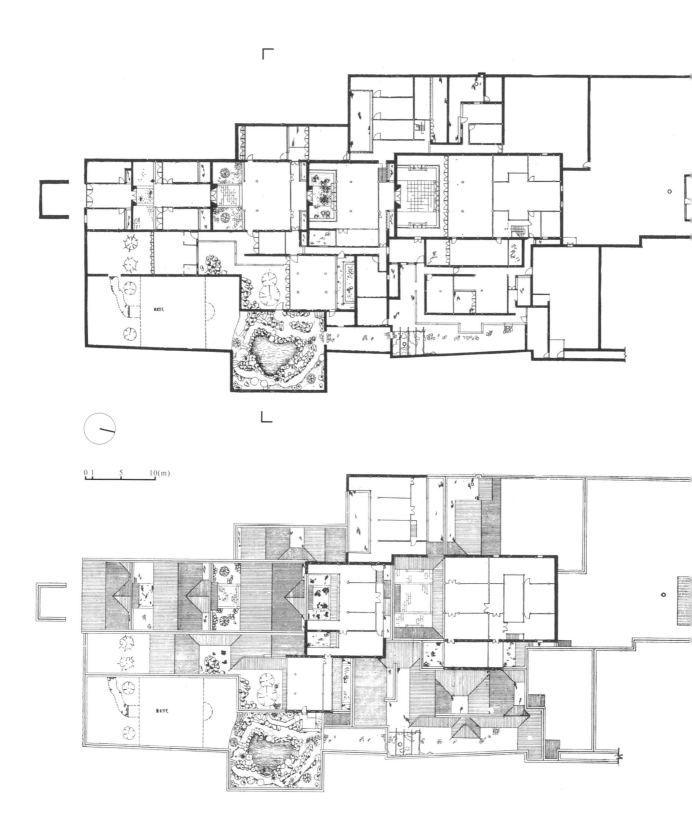

对页上：装驾桥巷吴宅一层平面图
对页下：装驾桥巷吴宅二层平面图
本页上：装驾桥巷吴宅花园剖面图

Opposite top: Ground floor plan of Wu's residence at Zhuangjiaqiao Alley
Opposite bottom: First floor plan of Wu's residence at Zhuangjiaqiao Alley
This page top: Section of garden of Wu's residence at Zhuangjiaqiao Alley

苏州住宅的平面，初看似甚简单，系由一进一进的封闭性院落形成，旁列避弄；然细审之则小院回廊、洞房曲户又使人如入迷楼，顿觉东西莫辨。从前人说中国旧建筑是中轴线左右对称，如进行具体分析，言均衡则可，言对称似觉太武断。这些旧住宅充分地应用因地制宜及合理安排的原则，在原有基础上扩建及改建时做到合理、经济，以符合当时生活需要。计成《园冶》所说"因地制宜"当然是总结前人经验而言，其影响及于后世于此可证。就调查所得，大至四条避弄，小至一个天井的住宅，虽变化多端，然为采光及空气流通起见，总不外乎是由下列各种与天井（院子）相连的单体建筑所组合成的。

The floor plan of Suzhou residences is formed by muliple stages of contained courtyards connected by Bilong on the side, which looks simple at first glance But with a closer look, one can become very disoriented and amazed upon entering the small courtyard with winding corridors and small buildings. It has been stated before that traditional Chinese architecture is always symmetrical along a central axis. This statement may be too subjective as the buildings are more balanced along the axis rather than simple in symmetry. These traditional residences are designed based on the principle of effectively using available land, and reasonable building layout. These residences are easily expandable or can be remodeled economically. The design and construction of the buildings should be in accordance with the living demands. The statement "build according to the condition of land" in Ji Cheng's *Yuanye* summarizes the experiences of many architects before, and its effect on forthcoming designers is very evident. It has been found during the survey that residences as large as those with four Bilong, or as small as those composed with only one courtyard may have many variations. But, all of these residences share a common feature that they are all formed in various combinations of single buildings with a courtyard as described in detail below.

阔街头巷网师园住宅部分内望

Inside of residential area of Wangshi Garden

第一类曲尺形，是类平面如单独成为一个住宅，则为小型住宅。其他如在正路两侧隙地建造者。甚至有因地形关系，不但建筑物作曲尺形，连天井亦有作曲尺形的。更有在主屋旁单面加厢或缀廊的，如东北街韩宅。但是如滚绣坊赵宅，在横长方形的大厅左面加廊，形成曲尺形，这种情况还是少见。

第二类横长方形或纵长方形，这类平面最为普通，各种厅堂及居屋皆用之。更有用两个横长方形的平面相对配置，中置天井，此即厅之前加一倒座，而不用厢或廊的，如史家巷彭宅。这种平面其前天井则为横长方形或方形，若为花厅则按园庭布置。建筑物有二面邻虚的、三面邻虚的与四面邻虚的。

第三类三合院，即主屋旁翼以两厢或二廊；更有主屋与倒座一面用厢或廊联系，如大儒巷潘宅小院；更有对照花厅，一面用廊联系，如铁瓶巷

The first category is a L-shaped layout. This forms a small residence if used alone. There are also houses built along small parcel of land along a cental axis in a larger residence. There can be such a case that both the courtyard and building are L shaped due to the size of the plot. In some cases a wing or a corridor is added to one side of the building such as in Han's residence on Dongbei Street. Zhao's residence at Gunxiu Fang adds a small corridor on the left side of a wide rectangular shaped hall to form a L shaped building which is rarely found.

The second category is that of wide or deep rectangular shape. This layout is most commonly seen for both halls and living quarters. There are those that have two wide rectangular shaped buildings facing each other with a courtyard in the center. This is having a reverse sited hall (Daozuo) in front of a hall with no wing, or corridor such as the Peng residence at Shijia Alley. The courtyard in this layout is either wide rectangular or square shaped. If this is a flower hall then the courtyard is laid out as a garden. The building can have windows opening on two, three or all four sides.

The third case is a Sanheyuan or three-side enclosed yard. This is where two wings or corridors are located by a main building, or even a main house is connected with a reverse facing building via a corridor or wing. The small courtyard of Pan's residence at Daru Alley is an excellent sample of this style. There are also cases where the two sections of a facing flower hall are connected with a corridor on one side of the hall such as the west flower hall of Ren's residence at Tieping Alley. The courtyard can be wide rectangular or even square shaped.

The fourth style is a Siheyuan or four side enclosed yard. Typically, a main building takes one side with two wings on each side of the main building, and a corridor completes the rectangle, such as Zhang's residence on Dongbei Street. There is also an instance that two facing main buildings are connected via corridors on both sides such as the facing flower hall of Chen's residence on Dongbei Street. In the case of Zoumalou, on all four sides are two-story buildings, such as Yang's residence on Jingde Road and Pan's residence on Nanshizhi Street. On the other hand the Peng's residence at Shijia Alley uses three corridors in front of a hall to form the Siheyuan.

The fifth case is a " 凸 " shaped layout. This style is formed either by building a Chuantang (a hall that built perpendicular to the main structure, written as 川堂 or 穿堂 in Chinese) behind a hall or adding a covered opera platform in front of the hall. If both structures are present, then this layout become cross shaped.

The sixth case is a " 工 " shaped layout. A corridor connects two halls along the central axis such as the main hall of Prince Zhong's Mansion on Dongbei Street. *Changwuzhi* states that the common peoples should avoid this shape because it looks like the official buildings, which is prohibited in the feudal age.

The seventh case is an " H " shaped layout, which is formed by joining two opposite facing Sanheyuan (see the third case). There are two wings both in front of and behind the main building such as Liu's residence at Xiaoxinqiao Alley (see pp. 64–65).

The eighth case is " 日 " shaped, which is formed by placing a Siheyuan (see case four) behind a Sanheyua (see case three) such as Pan's residence on Nanshizi Street (see pp. 48–49).

任宅西花厅。在这些情况下，天井有横长方形的，亦有方形的。

第四类四合院式。有一面主屋，左右列厢，对面用廊，如东北街张宅。有前后主屋，左右用廊，如东北街陈宅对照花厅。有四面作环楼的，江南称"走马楼"者，如景德路杨宅、南石子街潘宅皆是。而史家巷彭宅则厅前三面用廊，形成一个四合院。

第五类"凸"字形，即在厅后加川（穿）堂，或厅前正中置戏台，上覆廊。如二者并用则成"十"字形平面。

第六类"工"字形，即前后两厅间廊屋相联，如东北街太平天国忠王府正殿。《长物志》云："忌工字体，亦以近官廨也。"

第七类"H"形平面，用两个相反的三合院构成。即主屋翼以前后两厢，如小新桥巷刘宅（详见64—65页）。

第八类"日"形平面，即三合院之后加一个四合院连接而成，如南石子街潘宅（详见48—49页）。

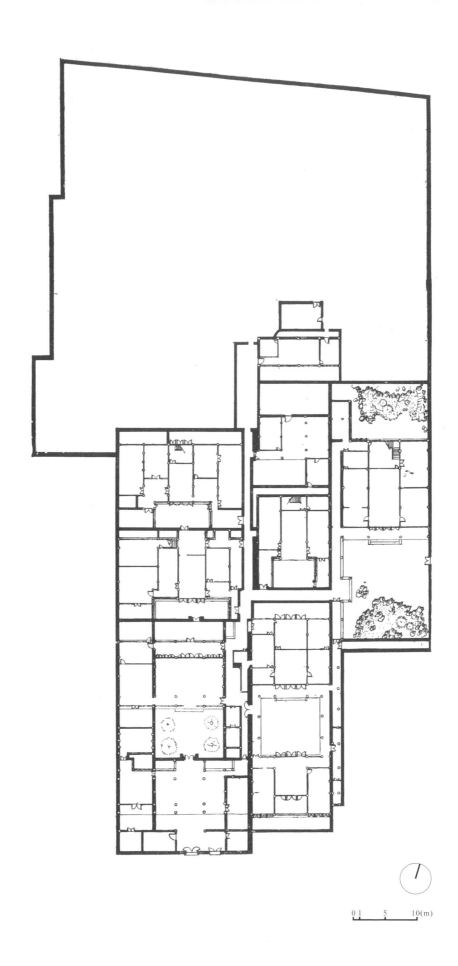

0 1　　　5　　　10(m)

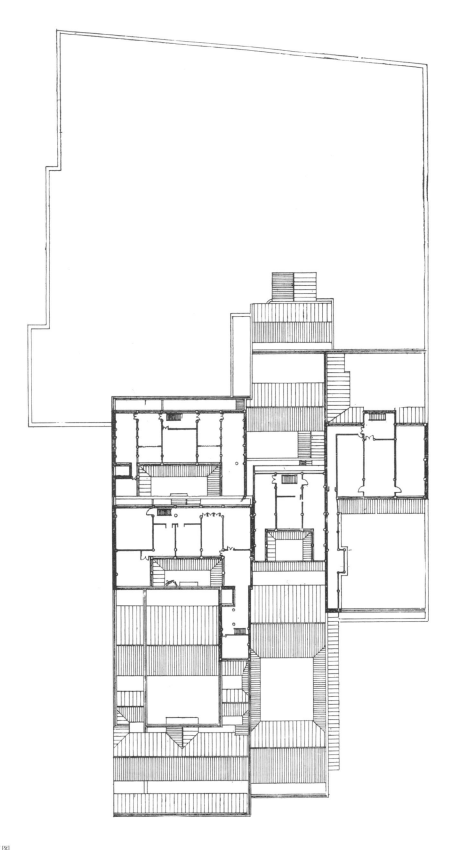

对页：东北街韩宅一层平面图
本页：东北街韩宅二层平面图

Opposite: Ground floor plan of Han's residence on Dongbei Street
This page: First floor plan of Han's residence on Dongbei Street

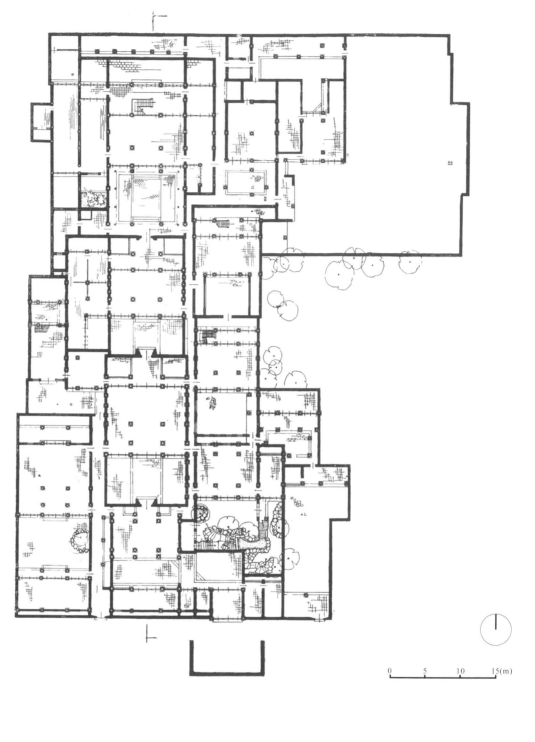

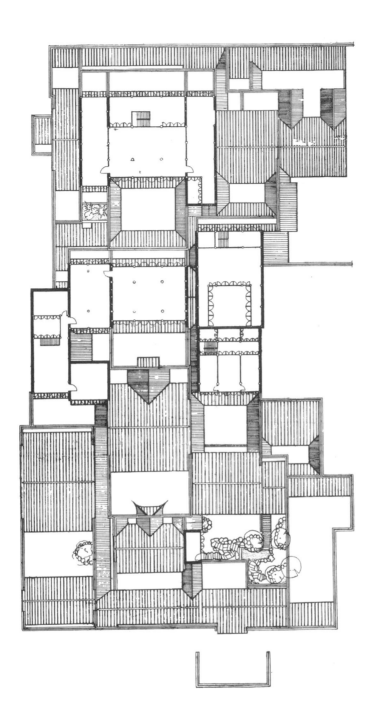

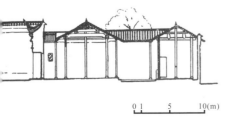

0 1 5 10(m)

对页上：史家巷彭宅一层平面图
本页上：史家巷彭宅二层平面图
下：史家巷彭宅剖面图

Opposite top: Ground floor plan of Peng's residence at Shijia Alley
This page top: First floor plan of Peng's residence at Shijia Alley
Bottom: Section of Peng's residence at Shijia Alley

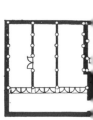

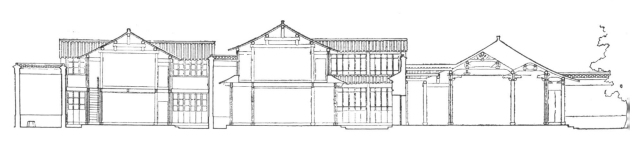

0 1 2 3(m)

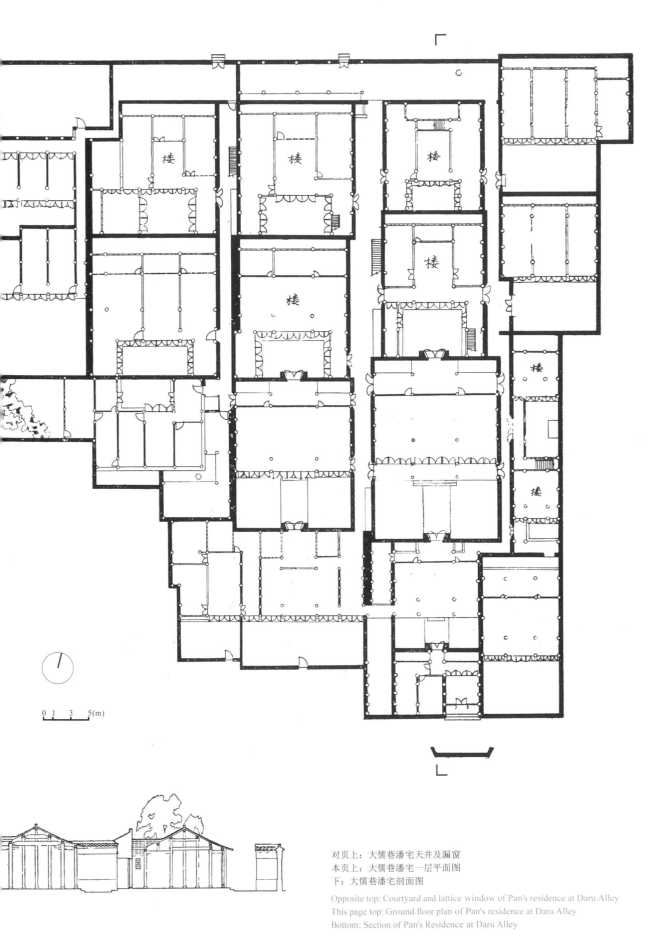

楼 楼 楼

楼

楼

楼

楼

楼

0 1 3 5(m)

对页上：大儒巷潘宅天井及漏窗
本页上：大儒巷潘宅一层平面图
下：大儒巷潘宅剖面图

Opposite top: Courtyard and lattice window of Pan's residence at Daru Alley
This page top: Ground floor plan of Pan's residence at Daru Alley
Bottom: Section of Pan's Residence at Daru Alley

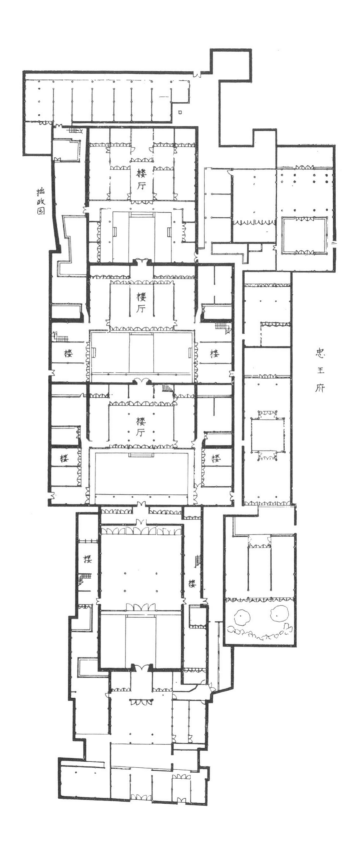

东北街张宅一层平面图

Ground floor plan of Zhang's residence on Dongbei Street

0 1   5   10(m)

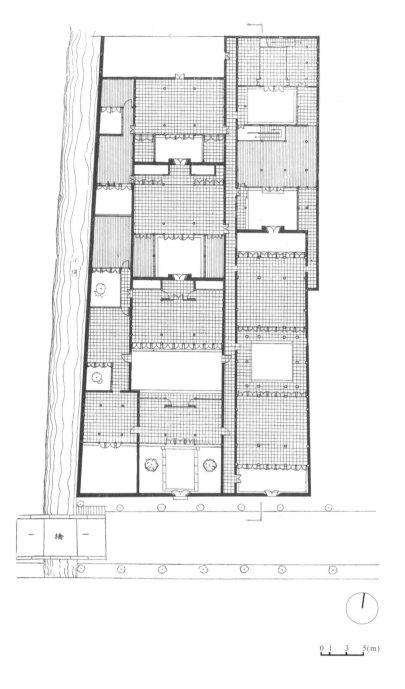

上：东北街陈宅一层平面图

下：东北街陈宅花厅剖面图

Top: Ground floor plan of Chen's residence on Dongbei Street

Bottom: Section of flower hall of Chen's residence on Dongbei Street

上：东北街太平天国忠王府剖面图
本页下：东北街太平天国忠王府大门
对页下：东北街太平天国忠王府平面图

Top: Section of Prince Zhong's Mansion
This page bottom: Main gate of Prince Zhong's Mansion
Opposite bottom: Ground floor plan of Prince Zhong's Mansion

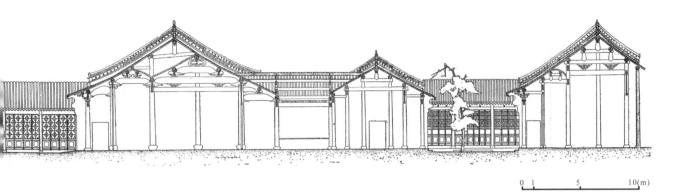

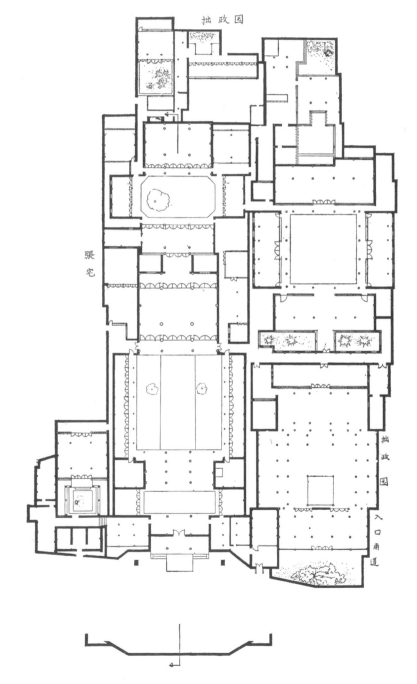

拙 政 园

张 宅

拙 政 园 入 口 甬 道

0 1   5   10(m)

0 1 5   10(m)

南石子街潘宅楼厅

Storied hall of Pan's residence on Nanshizi Street

除上述平面以外尚有两种变体：第一种如纽家巷潘宅花厅，俗称"纱帽厅"，即在横长方形的平面上在前凸出抱厦一间，实则《工段营造录》所谓"抱厦厅"，其后左右配两厢，构成凹形平面，以其似纱帽，故有此称。另一种如刘家浜尤宅，在天井中建一小阁，以代东厢，又用前后两个曲尺形合成"卝"形。因此将上述各单体根据不同的地形相配合，就组合成复杂多变的苏州旧住宅总平面。

苏州住宅平面的组合由以上各种单体配合而成，主要是为了符合当时封建社会的宗法观念的要求，充分表现了父父子子三纲五常的儒家思想。过去地主官僚在建造住宅时，极大多数向左右扩展，兼并他姓住宅，在原有旧建筑物的限制下，尽可能少变动，以避弄来作过渡，使中轴线得到正直。当然亦有例外的，如滚绣坊赵宅，便是前后厅事不在一中轴线上，这是很少见的。避弄除少数直的，差不多大部分是曲折的，其形成除上述原因外，在功能上是封建社会中女眷、仆从进出之处，文震亨《长物志》称它为"避弄"，殆即此意，谐吴人音为"备弄"，

There are two variations in addition to the eight styles mentioned above. The flower hall of Pan's residence at Niujia Alley is called Shamaoting in local slang. It adds a Baosha (a porch extended from the house or the small rooms connected with the porch) in front of a wide horizontal building. *Gongduan Yingzao Lu* defined it as Baoshating, which is a building with two wings behind it. This layout forms a " 凹 " shaped layout, and looks very similar to a type of gauze hat called Shamao (纱帽). You's residence at Liujiabang has a small pavilion built in the courtyard to substitue for the east wing, and uses two L-shaped layout to form a " 卝 " shape. The various single building shapes are placed in accordance with land plots to form the complex and ever changing layouts of Suzhou residences.

The formations of Suzhou residences consist of the various single unit layouts as mentioned above. The formation needs to meet the requirement of religious, social, and culture conception of a feudal society. It reflects the Sangang-Wuchang (the basis of Confucianism, stating family relatioinships in traditional Chinese society) and relationship between father and son that forms the core of Confucianism. The landlords and aristocrats typically expand their residences to the left and right by buying residences from other families. Its redesigning attempts to maintain the existing buidings as many as possible, and use Bilong (避弄) as transition points to keep a straight central axis. There are also some exceptions such as Zhao's residence at Gunxiu Fang whose front and rear halls are not on the same central axis. This type of exception is extremely rare. On the other hand it is very hard to find a straight Bilong. This is not only because they are used as transition between the various parts of a residence, but also because they are used as passageways for ladies and servants. In *Changwuzhi*(《长物志》) Wen Zhenheng called it Bilong to emulate the pronunciation of Beilong in the Wu dialect. It also acts as a passage for various houses of a large family. Small courtyards, studies, or small pavilions are constructed on small parcels of land to achieve balance along the central axis. A garden is built if the area is fairly large. The area of a small courtyard is usually the same as a Sanheyuan style building with the ratio of its depth to building height at approximately one. The width of the central bay in a three-bay building or the width of the central and side bay in a five-bay building determines the width of the courtyard. Large residence courtyards are typically wide rectangle shaped, and the depth of the wings is reduced accordingly. Corridors can be built instead of wings. The wide rectangular-shaped courtyards have greater width along the east west direction. This design can improve air circulation, reduce sunshining in summer and make an economic use of the land. The construction of both a front and a rear courtyard also greatly aids to keeping rooms cool during summer seasons by improving air movement. The rear courtyard can vary from 0.8 meter to 2 meters deep. Typically one to two trees are planted in the courtyard. A canopy can be raised during summer if there is no plant to shield people from the sun. The rear courtyard is also used for gutter drainage as well as air circulation. Walls in the rear are painted white, which improves the lighting in north facing rooms during winter via reflection. The planting of banana, parasol, or ivy on the walls during summer seasons provides a scene of greens. Narrow buildings such as studies or guest houses typically have deeper courtyards. The weather of this region is hot in summer, and mild in winter. The residential buildings are designed with increasing depth, and north facing rooms are very widely adapted. The north part of a Yuanyang (companion) hall, reverse seated buildings, or north facing rooms all contribute to the cooling during summer months.

其次亦大家庭各房进出之交通道。在解决中轴两侧不规则地形的问题时，其方法是置小院，造书房、精舍或小楼等，面积较大则建筑小花园。天井面积一般同三合院，其进深与建筑物高度为1:1；宽度三开间以明间面阔为准，或稍大；五开间以明间与次间面阔为准。大型住宅的天井以采取横长方形为多，并且将两厢进深减小，或易以两廊。天井作横长方形，东西长度大，其优点是在江南通风好，夏季日照少，用地亦经济。再以夏季炎热，复利用前后天井以利通风。后天井进深一般为2米左右，最小有为0.8米的。天井中皆植一二株乔木，如无种植，则于夏季搭凉棚来减少日照。后天井除用来通风外，且为檐滴落水之地。因为后墙粉白，冬季反射光可增加北房光线，夏日因天井中植有梧桐、芭蕉之属，或有绿色攀藤植物附于墙面之上，更觉满眼青翠。至于纵长方形的天井，一般是用在面阔较小的书斋、客轩之前。苏州因夏季较热，冬季不太冷，房屋进深比较深，其后部北向者，亦多可取之。而鸳鸯厅的北厅、倒座、北向房间等均发挥了令夏日凉爽的作用。

0 1　　　5　　　10(m)

本页上：刘家浜尤宅一层平面图
对页上：刘家浜尤宅二层平面图
下：刘家浜尤宅剖面图

This page top: Ground floor plan of You's residence at Liujiabang
Opposite top: First floor plan of You's residence at Liujiabang
Bottom: Section of You's residence at Liujiabang

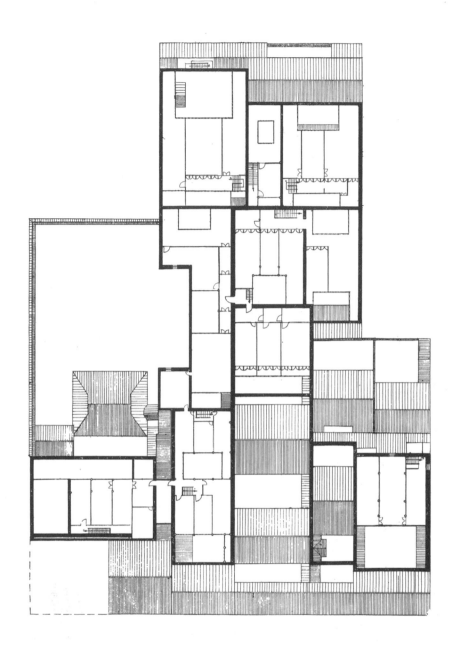

0 5 10 15(m)

上：纽家巷太平天国英王府（旧潘宅）纱帽厅
下：东北街太平天国忠王府二门

Top: Gauze hat hall of Prince Ying's Mansion (Pan's residence at Niujia Alley)
Bottom: The second gate of Prince Zhong's Mansion

纽家巷太平天国英王府纱帽厅（旧潘宅）陈设

Furnishing of gauze hat hall of Prince Ying's Mansion (Pan's residence
at Niujia Alley)

景德路杨宅花园入口

Entrance to the garden of Yang's residence on Jingde Road

仓米巷史宅半园入口

Entrance to Banyuan Garden of Shi's residence at Cangmi Alley

左上：阔街头巷某宅天井绿化
右上：西花桥巷潘宅三松堂前小院绿化
下：西花桥巷潘宅厢房天井绿化

Top left: Courtyard plants of a residence at Kuojietou Alley
Top right: Plants at the courtyard before Sansongtang of Pan's
residence at Xihuaqiao Alley
Bottom: Greenaries at the courtyard of Pan's residence at
Xihuaqiao Alley

庙堂巷畅园留云山房前

Front of Liuyunshanfang of Changyuan Garden

外影壁即照壁，过去系按官阶而定，有"一"字形的、"八"字形的、"冂"字形的，更有隔河的，必官至一品方能建造，如纽家巷潘宅、荫门彭宅的外影壁（潘世恩、彭启丰皆于清代官至大学士）。它起宅前屏障与对景作用，复饰有"鸿喜"之类吉祥字样，至于大门与外影壁之间的空间，则是作为车轿的回转道。内影壁，苏州用者不多，其目的亦为屏障作用。

中轴线的配置，大门一般在正中，对门有外影壁。早期的住宅如大儒巷丁宅、天官坊陆宅等，其平面犹属明制，大门皆在东南角。当然，清代的一些住宅亦有东南角开门的，如古市巷吴宅、史家巷彭宅，还未脱明代的影响，并且入内更有内影壁。有的于大门旁另辟偏门，如东北街张宅、梵门桥弄吴宅等。而宜多宾巷孔宅，其大门南向偏西，西白塔子巷李宅前半部建筑略侧，与后半部建筑不在一直线上，似与风水迷信有关。

The outer Yingbi (shadow wall) is also called Zhaobi (mirroring Wall). These were built according to one's rank in the government institutions. The styles of Zhaobi include " 一 " shaped, " 八 " shaped, " 冂 " shaped structures. There is even one built across the river, which is limited to the top ranking officials (Yiping) such as Pan's residence at Niujia Alley, and Peng's residence at Gate Feng. Both Pan Shi'en and Peng Qifeng were Prime Ministers during Qing dynasty. This structure provides a screen and a mirroring scene, and is decorated with characters associated with fortune such as 鸿 喜 (luck and happiness). The space between the Zhaobi and main gate is provided for carts to turn around. The inner Yingbi is not frequently used in Suzhou area, but provides a screen, too.

The placement along the central axis is formed as the following. The main gate is located on the central axis facing the exterior Yingbi. The early residences still follow a Ming dynasty style layout where the main gate is at the southeast corner such as Ding's residence at Daru Alley, and Lu's residence at Tianguan Fang. This style did also have an effect on some residences that were constructed during the Qing dynasty such as Wu's residence at Gushi Alley, and Peng's residence at Shijia Alley. There is even an interior Yingbi inside the main gate. A side door can also be found besides the main gate in certain instances such as Zhang's residence on Dongbei Street, and Wu's residence at Fanmenqiao Long. Kong's residence at Yiduobin Alley has its main gate facing south slightly by west. Front portion of Li's residence at Xibaitazi Alley is slightly off the central axis, and is not in one straight line with the rear sections of the residence. The reason may have to do with Fengshui (landscape geomancy).

上：东北街李宅隔河照壁
下：葑门彭宅隔河照壁

Top: Zhaobi of Li's residence on Dongbei Street
Bottom: Zhaobi of Peng's residence at Gate Feng

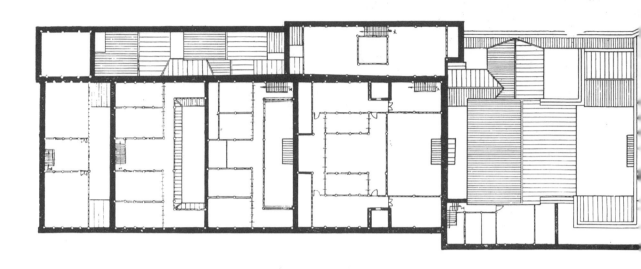

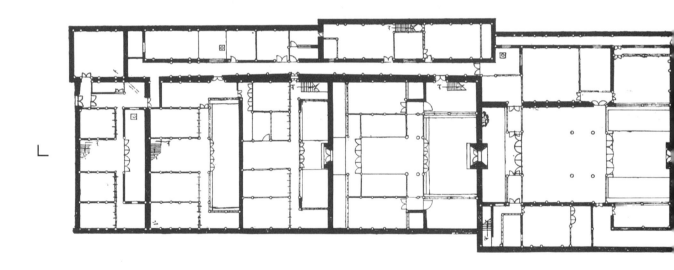

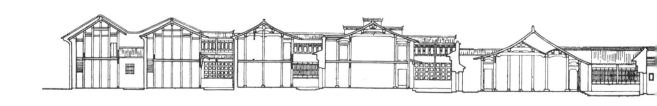

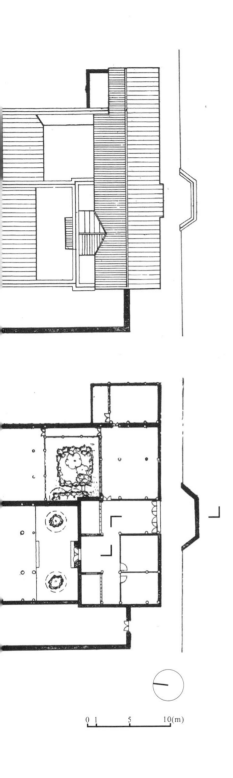

0 1   5   10(m)

上：大儒巷丁宅二层平面图
中：大儒巷丁宅一层平面图
下：大儒巷丁宅剖面图

Top: First floor plan of Ding's residence at Daru Alley
Middle: Ground floor plan of Ding's residence at Daru Alley
Bottom: Section of Ding's residence at Daru Alley

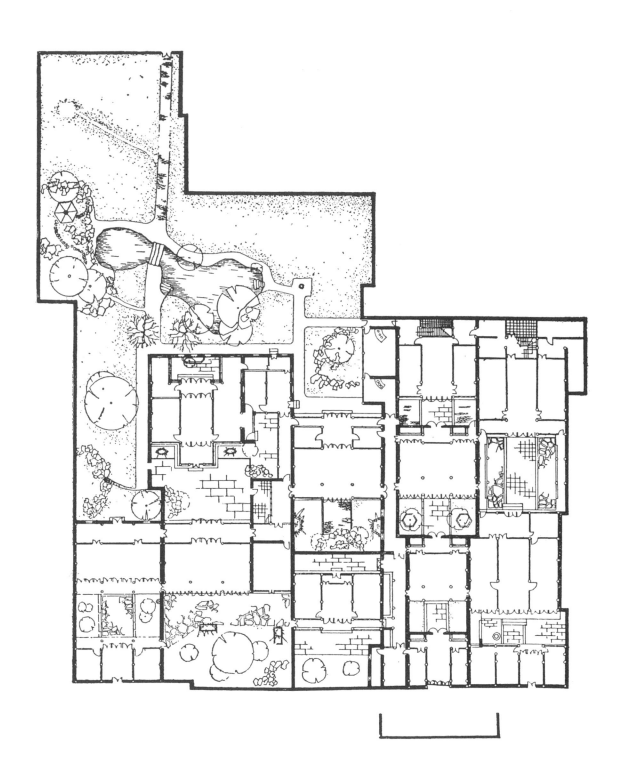

0 1   5   10(m)

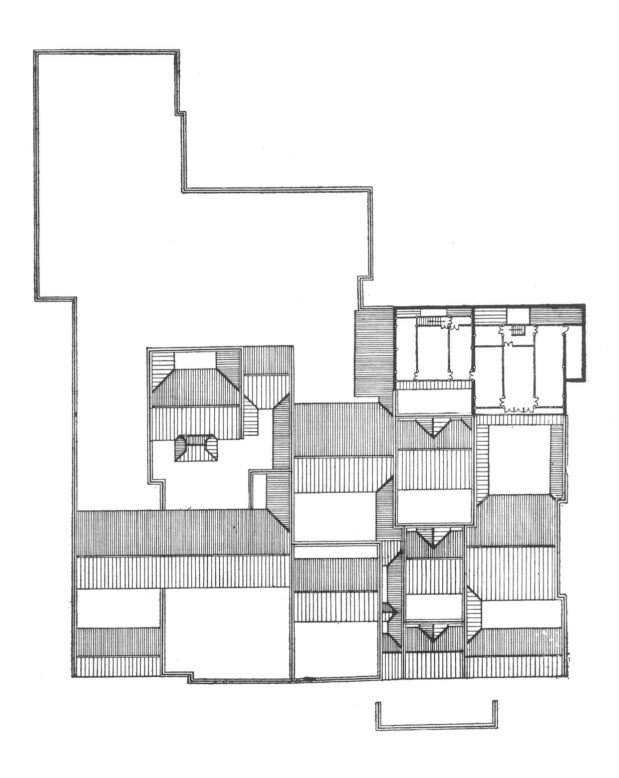

对页：宜多宾巷孔宅一层平面图
本页：宜多宾巷孔宅二层平面图

Opposite: Ground floor plan of Kong's residence at Yiduobin Alley
This page: First floor plan of Kong's residence at Yiduobin Alley

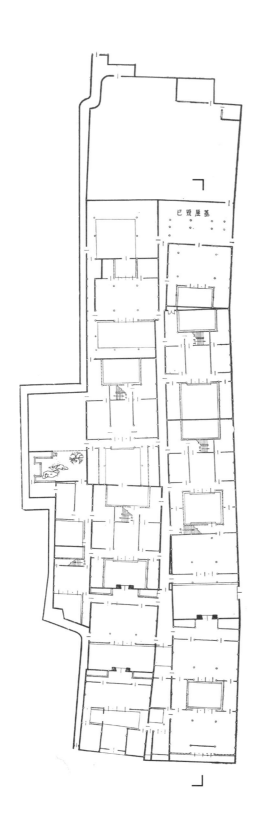

已毁屋基

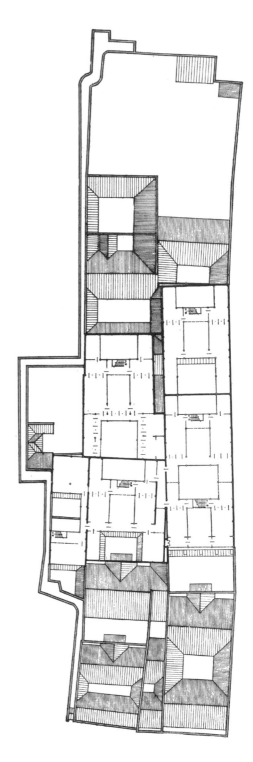

0 1   5   10(m)

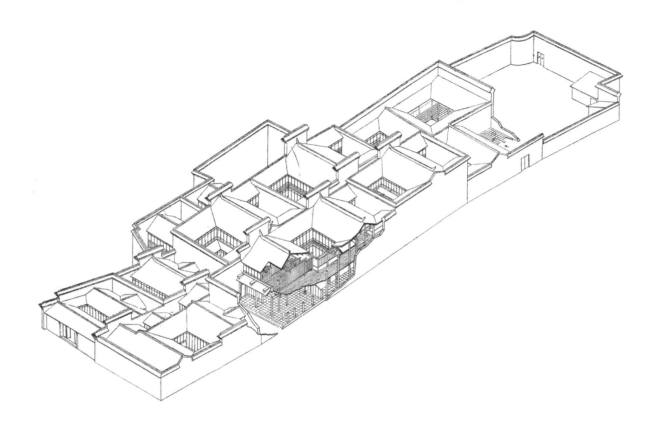

0 5(m)

对页左：西白塔子巷李宅一层平面图
对页右：西白塔子巷李宅二层平面图
本页上：西白塔子巷李宅轴测图
本页下：西白塔子巷李宅剖面图

Opposite left: Ground floor plan of Li's residence at Xibaitazi Alley
Opposite right: Frst floor plan of Li's residence at Xibaitazi Alley
This page top: Axonometric drawing of Li's residence at Xibaitazi Alley
This page bottom: Section of Li's residence at Xibaitazi Alley

对页：阔街头巷网师园东西辕门
本页：震泽县洞庭东山巷景

Opposite: Eastern and western Yuanmen of Wangshi Garden
This page: View of a lane in East Dongting Hill, Zhenze

自大门入，经门屋达轿厅（轿厅又称"茶厅"，为轿夫休息饮茶之处），皆敞口，无门窗。王洗马巷万宅轿厅虽在大门后，然大厅却在其左，不同置于一中轴线上，则为变例。轿厅旁有小院，其间建筑则作账房或家塾之用。经轿厅通过砖刻门楼，此种门楼一般用一面刻，早期官阶高者与后期豪奢之家者有用二面刻者，如天官坊陆宅、景德路杨宅。钱泳《履园丛话》云："又吾乡造屋，大厅前必有门楼，砖上雕刻人马戏文，玲珑剔透，尤为可笑。"足见门楼在清乾隆以前形制应较简朴，如东北街李宅（康熙时所建者）可证；时代越晚近越繁缛。至于门楼上的题字，按该处建筑物的类型不同而异，如大厅用"以介繁祉""清芬奕叶"等字。大厅乃供喜庆丧事及其他大典之用，面阔三间；但在大型住宅中，有的将架数增多，形成纵长方形的平面，因为一方面在功能需要上力求宏大，但另一方面又受制度限制，只好在深度上发展，亦权宜之计。

The place where sedan carriers take rest and drink tea is called Jiaoting meaning carriage hall, or tea hall. This structure immediately follows the gate house. Both gate house and carriage hall are buildings open on all four sides without doors or windows. The carriage hall of Wan's residence at Wangxianma Alley is directly behind the main gate, but the main hall is located to the left of carriage hall. This is an exception to the central axis alignment. There is typically a small courtyard by the carriage hall, and the buildings in this courtyard are either used as the clerks' room or a family school. Carved brick gate tower immediately follows the carriage hall. This type of gate tower usually employs a single side carving. The early period high level aristocrats' residences, and later luxurious houses may have gate towers carved on both sides such as Lu's residence at Tianguan Fang, and Yang's residence on Jingde Road. Qian Yong wrote in *Lüyuanconghua*(《履园丛话》), "The houses in my home town must include a gate tower in front of main hall. The bricks are carved with people and stories in a very fine fashion. The contents are extremely amusing." This statement shows that the gate tower built before Qianlong period in Qing dynasty is less gaudy. The Li's residence on Dongbei Street built during Kangxi period confirms this belief. Decorative carvings become exceedingly elaborate with time passing. The writings carved on the gate tower are changed according to the type of building that follows. Typically writings such as "以介繁祉" and "清芬奕叶" are used in main hall. The purpose of the main hall is for major ceremonies such as weddings and funerals. Main hall's width is about three bays, but can be extremely deep. The main hall of large residence has its depth increased, which makes the structure a long rectangle shape. This is because the function of the building requires it to be as large as possible, but the building codes at the time limits the width making increased depth the only alternative. The opera platform is placed in front of the main hall with small buildings along both sides of the main hall. The lower part of these side buildings are used as study, but the upper level side facing the side of the main hall (Shanmian or 山 面) has windows. These are the places for ladies to watch the opera performances. There can also be screen door on the side of the main hall instead of side buildings. These screen doors do not reach the floor, instead, they are fixed on walls that are covered with fine polished bricks. The screen doors can be removed and replaced with bamboo screens so that the places are adapted for ladies to watch the opera as in Pan's residence at Weidaoguanqian. The Nüting or masters' house (Shangfang) follows the main hall. This is a typical five-bay-wide building which can be separated into five or three rooms. The building is separated into three rooms by forming a center room that is three bays wide. Two wings are built on both sides of the building. A short wall can be used to separate the courtyard in front of and behind the building, so that the wing and end bay form an integral unit with its own independent courtyard for ladies to live in. If the secondary bay (Cijian) is separated to be a room, the end bay (Shaojian) can be used as a suite. If there is a suite inside a suite, then the room is known as a secret room such as the one in Peng's residence at Shijia Alley. The number of stages of masters' houses in a residence depends on the wealth of the owner. Servants' house or Piwu is always the final section of a residence, which is living area for female servants. The location of these buildings is typically one building in each stage, which is separated by a gate. This layout is very rigidly followed. All the masters' houses are grouped into a single section in some of the more recent constructions. There are also some

厅前置戏台。厅之两侧建小楼，下层为书房，在上层于厅堂山面梁架间有窗可启，该处即为女宾观剧处。亦有厅事两旁不建楼，而在山面置屏门，这些屏门并不到地，是装在水磨砖贴面的槛墙上，如将屏门除去，垂以竹帘，则为女宾观剧之处，如卫道观前潘宅。大厅后为女厅，亦称"上房"，大多数是面阔五间的楼厅，有分隔为五间的，有仅隔梢间、明间为三间厅的。两旁建厢楼，前后天井中亦有隔以短垣，使梢间与厢房自成一区，皆有独立小天井，便于女眷居住。如次间隔成房，则梢间成为套房，或套房内再加套房的，则称"密室"了，如史家巷彭宅。至于"上房"进数之多寡，则视主人财力而定，最后为"披屋"，亦称"下房"，为女仆居处。这些厅事排列，早期的是一进一门，很是规则；后期将上房部分独立成区（亦有从大厅便开始的，如景德路杨宅），周以高垣，以昭谨慎。其平面又多变化，有"H"形的、"曰"字形的，如铁瓶巷任宅、南石子街潘宅等。这些住宅建筑时皆不准备后代几房合居，待子孙支繁，则分宅而居，任、潘二宅即如此。任宅于西百花巷建新宅（任道熔之子，子木宅），潘宅系从纽家巷老宅分出者（老宅为潘世恩宅，分宅为其孙祖荫宅）。中型住宅只中轴一路，如增一路时，一般皆在东首，盖白虎首不能开口，必求在青龙首。如万不得已东侧无地可求时，在西首开门建屋时，必在东首略求一方之地，仅容开启一门亦为常见。如此目的不能求到，则设假门，或东首再置避弄，其前设门。用上述处理手法，则能于厅旁左右皆列门，达对称之目的。东西路建筑，最主要者当推花厅，为主人平时顾曲会宾之处，形式多变化，建筑亦精致。厅事为过去官僚地主用途丰富的建筑物。其标准：一、大厅之大小，以为百桌厅为尚。二、花厅之华奢，陈设之典雅。三、砖刻门楼之精细。四、女厅（上房）之高畅。

residences that put main hall into the residence section such as Yang's residence on Jingde Road. All four sides of the masters' house section are surrounded by high walls in order to be prudent about security and safety. The floor plan can have variations like " H " shape or " 曰 " shape. Ren's residence at Tieping Alley, and Pan's residence on Nanshizi Street are all good examples of this type. These residences are not built for all members of several generations of the family to live in the same residence. When the family has extended its size, some of the family memberrs may branch out to live at other locations, which is the case for both Ren's and Pan's residences. The Ren family built a new residence at Xibaihua Alley, which is taken by Ren Daorong's son Zimu. Pan's residence is branched out from the old residence at Niujia Alley. The original residence was that of Pan Shi'en, and the new residence belonged to the grandson Pan Zuyin. Medium residences may only have one axis of buildings. The addition of a new axis to a residence must be on the east side because the mouth connot be opened on the white tiger (west) side, and must be on the azure dragon (east) side. In case there is no space available for expansion on the east side, it is prudent to seek a small plot of land on the east side just to open a door. This practice is quite common. If it is impossible to open a door, then the option is either to build a fake door, or to place a Bilong on the east side with a door opening at the end. By using the above techniques it is possible to open doors on both sides of the hall to achieve symmetry. The most important building on the east or west axis is Huating (flower hall). This is the place where the host greets his guests and enjoys music. The style can vary dramatically, and the buildings are extremely ornate. These halls are for the aristocrats to demonstrate their wealth. The comparison is based on four aspects. First is the size of the main hall, and the best is the hall that can hold a hundred tables. Second is the luxury of the flower hall, and the elegance of its decoration. Third is the finesse of carved brick gate towers. Forth is the height and openness of Nüting (masters' house). Flower hall has several different styles of construction. The facing flower hall has two structures that are facing each other with front on the north and south side. This is seen in both Shi's residence at Cangmi Alley, and Chen's residence on Dongbei Street. The east west flower halls can be found in Ren's residence at Tieping Alley. The companion flower hall is one structure, where both the south and north sides can be front of the building. This type of flower hall is very common in Suzhou. The free standing flower hall is also very common in Suzhou. There are also cases where library is built right behind the flower hall such as Liu's residence at Xiaoxinqiao Alley, and Gu's residence at Tieping Alley. Small gardens are usually built in front of and/or behind the flower hall based on the size and shape of the land. There are also small halls and storied buildings constructed for living areas. Piwu (披 屋) is built in unoccupied small spaces for storage or as living area for female servants. These spaces can also be used to build family altar where the ancestors are remembered. In the past there were residences that built multiple sections of small halls on the east and west side of main residence and rented these halls to reserve government officials such as Wu's residence at Fanmenqiao Long. The kitchen and kitchen workers' residence are always at the end of a side axis near the rear gate, and is separated by high walls for fire safety. There is also storage built nearby for firewood and rice. This planning makes it possible to prevent the cooking fume from flowing into the living areas, which refelcts the

花厅种类有："对照花厅"，即南北二花厅相对而建者，如仓米巷史宅、东北街陈宅等；"东西花厅"，如铁瓶巷任宅；"鸳鸯花厅"，即一厅内南北二向皆作正面者，苏州此例甚多；"独立式花厅"，亦为常见。更有花厅后建藏书楼者，如小新桥巷刘宅、铁瓶巷顾宅。至于花厅前后的布置，则按地形设计成小型园林，除花厅外，又可安排一些小型厅堂及楼屋以充居住之用，间有于隙地建披屋为下房或兼作储藏杂物之用，亦有列家祠以供牌位的。过去曾有若干住宅于东西两侧建逐进小厅，用以出租予候补官员，如梵门桥弄吴宅者。厨房及厨工住处类皆在偏路之后，邻近后门，周以围墙，单独成区，以防火患，并附以柴房，就近且设谷仓。再如此安排，可使炊事油腥之气不入居住部分，即孔子所谓"君子远庖厨也"。厨工皆为男性，不得与女眷相居一处。再若门房、轿班、账房、仆从、塾师、清客等他姓男子，亦一律皆生活于居住部分之外，与上房隔绝。这些充分体现并巩固封建礼教在建筑中的独特影响。

避弄是夹在两路建筑物中的夹弄，或单路建筑物旁的通道，为苏州旧住宅中引人注目的地方。阴暗深远，狭窄如幽巷，其功能为直接联系两旁建筑物，在建筑群中具重要位置。宽度最小者仅可通一人，阔者可通一轿。采光方法有：一、避弄中沿墙之狭小天井；二、酌开天窗；三、弄侧墙上漏窗之侧面光；四、进口、出口之光线与通两旁建筑物的门道光线，在夜间，则于墙面壁龛内置油灯照明。因避弄内有曲折的通道，有旁列天井，间或通过楼屋下层，以致屋顶结构极为错综复杂。

Confucius saying, "A gentleman should keep away from kitchen." The kitchen workers are always male, and cannot live in the same area as the ladies. Other male employees including doormen, sedan carriers, clerks, servants and family school instructors, and even the inner house guests (Qingke, written as 清客 in Chinese, guests that entertains and studies with the male owners of the house) all live outside the family living areas, which is completely separated from where the masters' houses are located. This both represents and emphasizes the role of feudalistic social order in residence design and construction.

Bilong is the passageway that exists between two building complexes, or the passageway beside an axis of buildings. This is a very intriguing part of Suzhou residence. Its length, darkness, and narrowness all give it a gloomy appearance. Its function is to connect buildings on the sides, and is a very important part of building complex. The widest Bilong can allow a sedan to path, while the narrowest will only allow the passage of a person. The lighting can come from four sources. First source is the small courtyards that come out from the side of buildings. Building skylights is another source for lighting. The third is from lattice windows built on walls. Forth and not least is light from the ends of the passageway as well as those from doorways along the passage. There are also small niches on the wall where oil lights can be placed for night illumination. These passageways can be twisting and turning with courtyards, or even going through lower floors of storied buildings making the roof structure extremely complex.

东北街李宅花厅

Flower hall of Li's residence on Dongbei Street

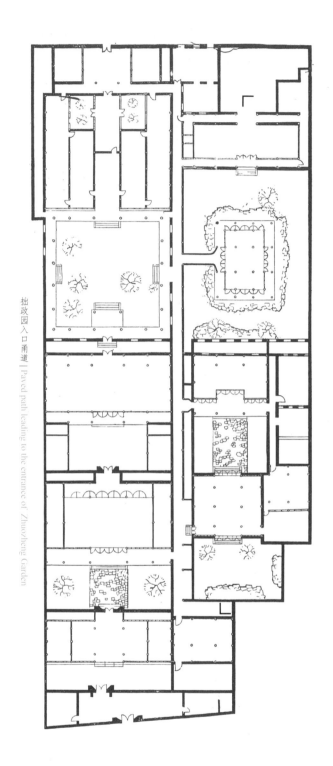

拙政园入口甬道 | Paved path leading to the entrance of Zhuozheng Garden

0 1   5   10(m)

河流 | River

本页左：东北街李宅一层平面图
上：东北街李宅花园东路剖面图
下：东北街李宅避弄

This page left: Ground floor plan of Li's residence on Dongbei Street
Top: Section of east axis of Li's residence on Dongbei Street
Bottom: Bilong of Li's residence on Dongbei Street

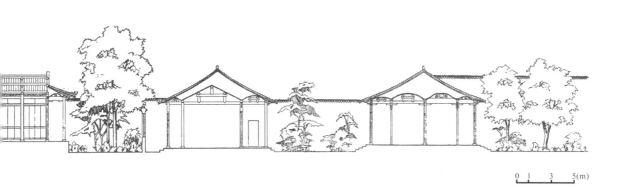

0 1   3   5(m)

上：震泽县洞庭东山某宅砖刻门楼
下：震泽县洞庭东山某宅砖刻门楼

Top: Brick carving over a gate tower of a residence in East Dongting Hill, Zhenze
Bottom: Brick carving over a gate tower of a residence in East Dongting Hill, Zhenze

景德路杨宅大厅门楼

Gate tower of main hall of Yang's residence on Jingde Road

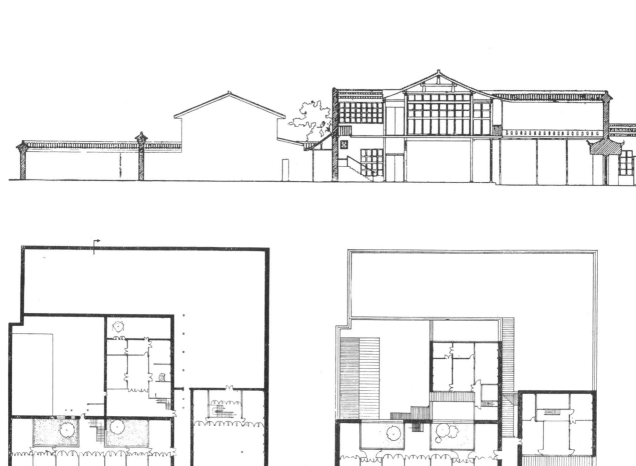

0 1   5   10(m)

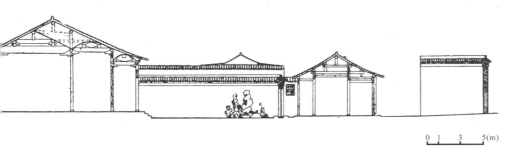

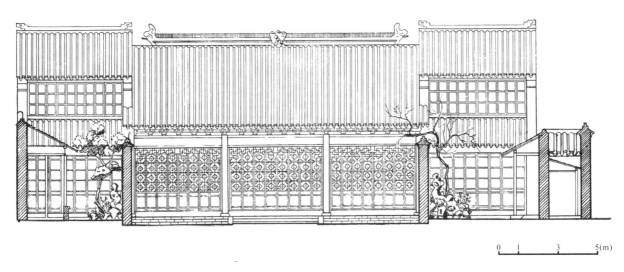

上：西百花巷颜宅剖面图
对页左下：西百花巷颜宅一层平面图
对页右下：西百花巷颜宅二层平面图
本页下：西百花巷颜宅大厅立面图

Top: Section of Yan's residence at Xibaihua Alley
Opposite bottom left: Ground floor plan of Yan's residence at Xibaihua Alley
Opposite bottom right: First floor plan of Yan's residence at Xibaihua Alley
This page bottom: Elevation of main hall of Yan's residence at Xibaihua Alley

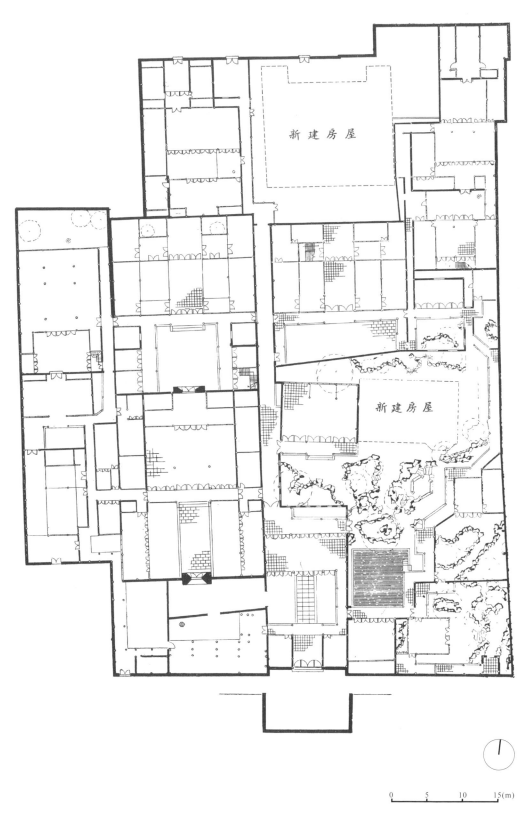

新建房屋

新建房屋

0　　　5　　　10　　15(m)

王洗马巷万宅一层平面图

Ground floor plan of Wan's residence at Wangxianma Alley

132

王洗马巷万宅二层平面图

First floor plan of Wan's residence at Wangxianma Alley

上：天官坊陆宅明代须弥座
左下：卫道观前潘宅大厅女宾观剧处
右下：卫道观前潘宅槅扇（门）

Top: Carved base of Ming dynasty of Lu's residence at Tianguan Fang
Bottom left: Opera-viewing site for ladies at Pan's residence at Weidaoguanqian
Bottom right: Lattices doors of Pan's residence at Weidaoguanqian

东北街李宅二门

The second gate of Li's residence on Dongbei Street

上：东北街张宅厢楼
下：西花桥巷潘宅厢楼

Top: Wing building of Zhang's residence on Dongbei Street
Bottom: Wing building of Pan's residence at Xihuaqiao Alley

上：纽家巷太平天国英王府（旧潘宅）纱帽厅后厢房
下：卫道观前杨宅小天井

Top: Back wing-room of gauze hat hall of Prince Ying's Mansion (Pan's residence at Niujia Alley)
Bottom: A small courtyard of Yang's residence at Weidaoguanqian

上：景德路杨宅楼厅
下：西花桥巷潘宅厢楼

Top: Storied hall of Yang's residence on Jingde Road
Bottom: Wing building of Pan's residence at Xihuaqiao Alley

上：东北街李宅花厅
下：大石头巷吴宅花厅

Top: Flower hall of Li's residence on Dongbei Street
Bottom: Flower hall of Wu's residence at Dashitou Alley

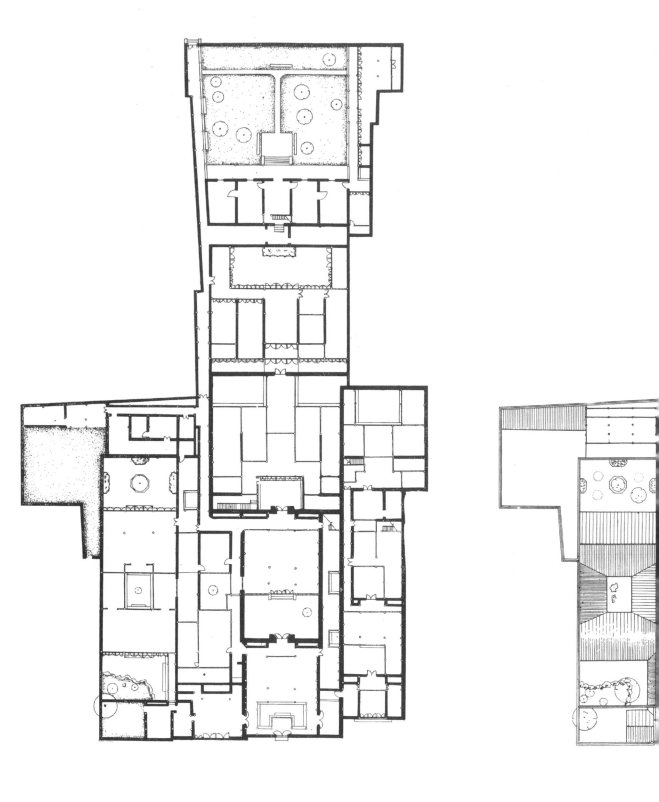

0 1　　5　　10(m)

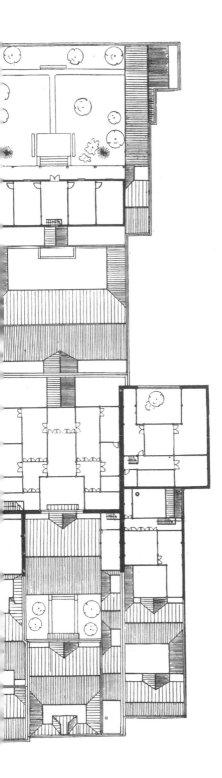

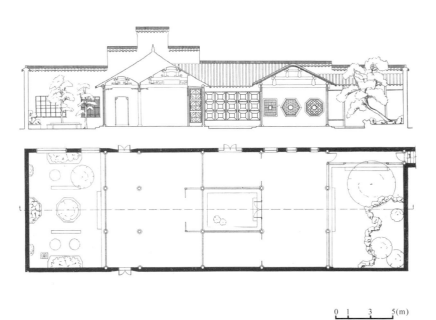

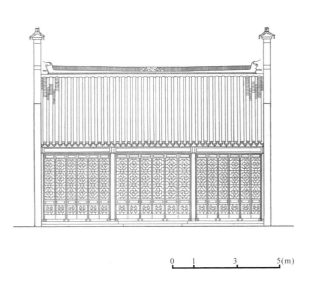

对页：大石头巷吴宅一层平面图
跨页：大石头巷吴宅二层平面图
本页上：大石头巷吴宅花厅平面图及剖面图
本页下：大石头巷吴宅花厅立面图

Opposite: Ground floor plan of Wu's residence at Dashitou Alley
Cross page: First floor plan of Wu's residence at Dashitou Alley
This page top: Floor plan and section of flower hall of Wu's residence at Dashitou Alley
This page bottom: Elevation of flower hall of Wu's residence at Dashitou Alley

本页：仓米巷史宅大门
对页上：仓米巷史宅半园平面图
对页下：仓米巷史宅剖面图

This page: Front gate of Shi's residence at Cangmi Alley
Opposite top: Floor plan of Shi's residence and Banyuan Garden at Cangmi Alley
Opposite bottom: Section of Shi's residence at Cangmi Alley

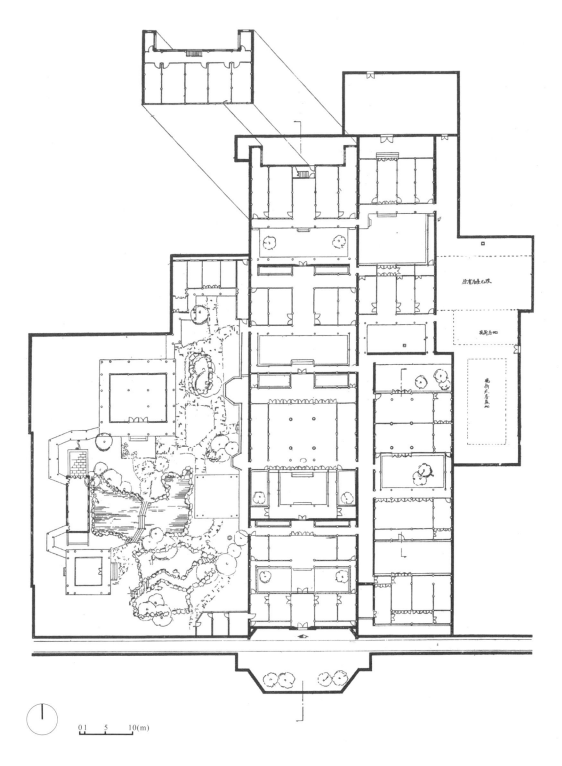

0 1　　5　　10(m)

0 1　　5　　10(m)

上：东北街拙政园三十六鸳鸯馆内陈设
下：西花桥巷潘宅内部陈设

Top: Furnishings at Thirty-Six Pairs of Mandarin Ducks Hall of
　　Zhuozheng Garden
Bottom: Furnishing at Pan's residence at Xihuaqiao Alley

上：东北街李宅漏窗
左下：大儒巷潘宅避弄漏窗
右下：史家巷彭宅天井

Top: Lattice window of Li's residence on Dongbei Street
Bottom left: Lattice window of Bilong of Pan's residence at Daru Alley
Bottom right: Courtyard of Peng's residence at Shijia Alley

在苏州，旧住宅多半用高墙封闭。围墙为水平形，露出屋顶一部分。山墙形式有硬山式：山墙不出头，循着屋顶坡度作"人"字形，是比较简陋的建筑用之。一般山墙皆高出屋面以上，做成梯级形式的"五山屏风墙"，因可以防火，故又称"封火墙"。更有以前二者混合而用，以水平形围墙相连，露出屋顶一部分，外观错落有致。山墙后期亦有做成观音兜者。天井的深度与屋高比例，在小型住宅有不到1:1的。其沿街之墙，上部往往用瓦花墙（瓦砌漏窗），或用琉璃预制漏窗，以利内部房屋采光与通风。

外墙面墁石灰，有刷青煤作灰黑色的，亦有存石灰本色的。因为外墙墁石灰，屋顶覆盖灰色蝴蝶瓦，木料又棕黑色或栗色，配以柔和的轮廓线，予人以雅洁的感觉。唯苏州旧住宅在外墙水作部分不十分重视，而内部装修布置则踵事增华，与附近无锡富商住宅讲究外观以炫富者有所不同。

Traditional Suzhou residences are usually enclosed with high walls. These walls can be level, with a portion of the roof on display. The full gable (Yingshan) style walls are slightly lower than the roof of the house, and form a "人" shape on top. This is mostly used for simple low cost buildings. Walls along both sides of the building (Shanqiang side) are typically taller than the roof and are in a staircase shape. This style is called Wushanpingfengqiang (a wall that is staircase shaped, and has five steps going up and down, also known as staircase shaped). This is also known as a firewall for its ability to slow the spread of fire from residence to residence. A combination of the two styles mentioned above, with level walls as transition is widely used in various buildings. A small section of the roof is sometimes displayed intentionally a sense of pleasing asymmetry from the outside. Guanyindou (a full gable wall higher than the building roof, and with a softened outline) is another commonly used style. The ratio of courtyard depth to building height can be less than one in small residences. The walls along streets are often decorated with lattice windows made from tile or prefabricated porcelain material to enhance lighting and airflow of buildings.

The exterior walls are covered with a lime-based stucco. The walls can be painted in a dark gray color, or kept in the white color of lime. The combination of white wall, dark grey roof tiles, with grey or brown colored wood along a soft outline provides a clean and pleasing exterior. The outside wall painting and decoration of traditional Suzhou residences are kept in a very simple style, but the interior decoration can become extremely elaborate, and exquisite. This style is in stark contrast with residences at nearby Wuxi, which place a heavy emphasis on exterior decoration.

The main gates are usually formed by six pieces of wood panels, but smaller residences may use four panels instead. Bamboo strips were also used to build doors during early Qing dynasty. Bamboo strings and thin strips of lead were all material used to decorate the wood plank doors. Half height door is another style continuing to use. There is even two-story gate house with windows on the upper level on purpose of defence and guard. This style is often seen in the villages south of Suzhou City, especially those along East and West Dongting Hills region, as well as some towns in Ningbo and Shaoxing. The general's door (Jiangjunmen 将军门) of early Ming periods consists of two large door leaves along with two drum shaped base stones. The stones are carved with lotus and nine lions. Four door pegs are placed on these doors. A large screen wall (Zhaobi) with carriage doors (Yuanmen) on both sides form rest of the entrance. The stone framed gate (Shikumen) style appeared much later in Suzhou, and is mainly used among small residences. Windows are placed beside the doors to provide lighting for both wings. There is also flying panels decorating the door like those used at Liu's residence located at Liaojia Alley. There is rarely any window opening on walls along the side of the house. The windows are typically rectangular, or polygon shaped, and are harmonious with the staircase shaped walls. There are many small niches with very intricate

住宅大门普通为板门六扇，小者亦有四扇的。古式（清中叶前旧住宅）有用竹丝作格门形状者，更有板门外钉竹片呈图案形状者，晚近易用铅皮以代竹片。矮挞门间有仍沿用者，更有门屋作楼层者，大门之上系楼窗，此种形式常见于苏南村镇，而尤以洞庭东西山为多（浙江宁绍村镇亦有之），其用意在防御盗贼及观望之用。早期府第之称"将军门"者则用大门两扇，佐以砷石（抱鼓石），砷石以刻九狮荷叶盘者最高贵。门上施阀阅（门簪）四枚，前用大照壁及东西辕门。石库门在苏州是比较晚期的，多数用在小型住宅、其两旁间有开窗者，俾使左右双厢受到南薰。除上述几种大门形式外，并有在大门上施门罩的，如廖家巷刘宅便是一例。山墙上开窗者甚少，有之亦甚小，其形式作方形或多边形，它与梯级形的山墙配合得很协调。有些沿街的外墙上有灯龛，凹入墙内，外饰以小罩，很玲珑，系置路灯所在。在宅内每一进分隔皆有大门，上砌华丽的砖刻门楼。门之向外一面钉水磨方砖，用以防火防盗。方砖皆正置，每块钉四，更有向内一面加钉铁皮的，不多见。一般皆钉铁板数条。至于边门、后门做法相同，边门则用门一扇。厅堂两侧通避弄的，用板门两扇，正面（向厅堂一面）髹白漆，加铜制门饰，门框上部冠刻砖题字，门扇上书门对。如逢喜庆及典礼，将该宅中轴线上前部诸门尽启，直达大厅，自外望内，厅堂重叠，在平面上给人以极深远的感觉。巨室外墙更置有系马环者。

covers located along walls. These niches are used for placing street lighting. Doors with intricate carved brick frames are opening every two stages in a residential compound. The outside is covered with fine polished bricks nailed to the door frame for fire prvention and being theftproof. The inside can be covered with metal sheets if desired by the resident. This usually involves several thin strips of metal nailed to the door. The rear and side doors of a residence are constructed in the same fashion. The side door usually consists of one piece of wood plank. Two plank doors are usually used for halls and lounges that have access to side passages (Bilong). The front side (inside) is painted white with copper decorative devices. There are characters carved on the brick placed on top of doorframe. There are also antithetical couplets placed on the doors. All doors along the central axis leading to the main hall are opened during celebration and major ceremonies. They look deep and serene from the outside. This is the proper effect of lining all buildings along a central axis. For large residences there is usually rings placed on outside walls for tying horses.

阔街头巷某宅漏窗

Lattice window of a residence at Kuojietou Alley

上：阔街头巷网师园大门
下：狮子林大门

Top: Main gate of Wangshi Garden
Bottom: Main gate of Shizilin

震泽县洞庭东山街巷某宅大门

Main gate of a residence in East Dongting Hill, Zhenze

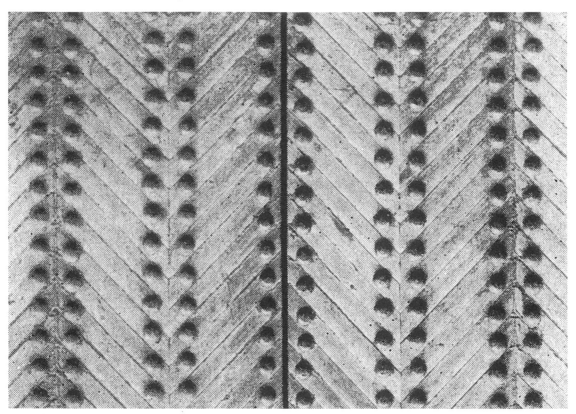

上：悬桥巷潘姓祠堂竹片大门
下：大儒巷丁宅竹片大门

Top: Bamboo gate of Pan's family altar at Xuanqiao Alley
Bottom: Bamboo gate of Ding's residence at Daru Alley

卫道观前潘宅竹片大门

Bamboo gate of Pan's residence at Weidaoguanqian

阔街头巷网师园大厅门楼

Gate tower of main hall of Wangshi Garden

154

左上：史家巷彭宅贴砖偏门
左下：纽家巷太平天国英王府纱帽厅（旧潘宅）门对

右上：史家巷彭宅贴砖大门
右下：铁瓶巷顾宅砖框门

Top left: Brick-covered side gate of Peng's residence at Shijia Alley
Bottom left: Couplet on a door at gauze hat hall of Prince Ying's Mansion (Pan's residence at Niujia Alley)

Top right: Brick-covered main gate of Peng's residence at Shijia Alley
Bottom right: Door with brick frame of Gu's residence at Tieping Alley

上：南石子街潘宅拴马环
下：铁瓶巷顾宅门饰

Top: Ring to hold horse bridle of Pan's residence on Nanshizi Street
Bottom: Door decoration of Gu's residence at Tieping Alley

阔街头巷网师园大门抱鼓石

Drum shaped base stone of Wangshi Garden

建筑构造、装饰及其他 | Construction, Decoration, and Others

　　苏州旧住宅在建筑构造与装饰等方面自有其独具的形式与风格，为苏南建筑的代表，其所及范围包括整个太湖流域。特征在柔和、雅洁，即吴语所谓"糯"者。兹将各部分分述于下：

　　墙　外墙一般高约 6 米，厚 42 厘米左右，除在安全上起防卫作用外，并用以防火，对隔音亦起很大作用，可分为实砌墙、空斗（心）墙及下实上空的混合墙三种。墙用石条砌成墙脚（裙肩）部分，其上用砖实砌。砌法有平砌，亦有横直间砌，大多是用三横三直。普通外墙下半部用实砌，上半部用空斗。墙面极少开窗，粉饰一般用石灰，外墙有加青煤的。至于住宅内部之墙面，皆为白色，室内更有用白蜡打磨若镜面者，即《园冶》所谓"镜面墙"。以水磨砖贴壁整面，或壁之下半部分，即《长物志》所指"四壁用细砖砌者佳，不则竟用粉壁"。

　　地面　天井地面有墁石板的，有铺冰裂纹石块的，有用鹅子石或与缸片铺作图案形状的，有用仄砖铺的，石片间缸片铺的，皆富于变化，用来增加天井的美观。建筑物内部墁砖，

The traditional Suzhou residences have unique styles in construction and decoration. This style is typical in south Jiangsu province, which includes the entire Taihu Lake region. This style is characterized by simplicity and elegance. It is called Nuo (糯) in Wu dialect.

Wall

The exterior walls are generally six meters high and 42 centimeters thick. This wall provides security, fire prevention, and noise insulation. The walls can be built in the following three styles: filled solid, hollow, and mixed half hollow (top) and half solid (bottom). Stone slabs form the base of walls (Qunjian), and bricks are stacked on top. The bricks are stacked horizontally or in a mixed horizontal and vertical fashion. The mixed stacking is formed in pattern of three horizontal and three vertical bricks. The commonly seen outside walls are filled solid on the bottom and hollow in the center on top. The walls have few windows, and painted with lime-based stucco. Black coal powder can be used as a pigment to color exterior walls if desired. The interior walls are always kept in a white color. The use of polished wax on walls to a mirror like quality forms the so called mirror-wall as defined in *Yuanye*. The wall can be covered entirely with fine polished bricks, or at least the lower half. The book *Changwuzhi* states, "The walls decorated with polished bricks are the best. The other option is to paint the wall white."

Floor

The courtyard floors can be paved with stone slabs, ice crack patterned stone, pebbles mixed with crushed porcelain pieces to form patterns, bricks in herringbone pattern, and crushed stones mixed with crushed porcelain. These materials can be varied to form various patterns creatively to enhance the beauty of courtyard. The interior floors are covered with bricks. The floor foundation is a compacted lime and soil mixture. The square bricks are laid on top, and sand can be spread beneath the bricks. The bricks can be laid elaborately by putting four inverted jars at each corner of every brick piece and filling the brickwork joints with sand. This is the same construction style used in Huizhou and Yangzhou area. The suspended floors with open area underneath the stone slabs are also used. These construction styles all focus on the purpose of moisture isolation. The bedroom floor is covered with bricks and has a wood floor (floor screen) constructed on top during winter. The wood floor is constructed with wood planks that are 3.5 centimeters thick with three joists placed below. Four short legs support the edges of each plank. The planks are one meter wide, and 1.3 meters long and can be placed freely according to the room size. The number of planks in a room is dependent on its depth and width. Planks are placed every five Chi (1.6 meters) along the depth of a building. The height of each piece is approximately 3 centimeters beneath the top of the stone drums used to support the columns. *Changwuzhi* points out, "Floor screen can be used, ... but it is not as elegant as fine bricks. The south part of China is very humid and suspended placement works best. The only drawback is the expense." The use of Sanhetu (mixed earth) or use of lime compacted on existing soil floor without brick cover are all due to economical concerns. These types of floor are mostly used in storage and kitchen areas. There is also the addition of salt to soil to form the floor. The Chapter of Residences of Li Yu's *Yijiayan* has record of using irregular shaped rough bricks to form ice break, and turtle back patterns. The brick and compacted floors cannot provide long term moisture insulation, and wood floors are best for common households.

其做法是土加石灰夯实，其上铺砂，墁方砖，亦有不铺砂者。讲究者在方砖下四角倒置四瓮，隙间填砂，徽州、扬州其法相同，复有方砖下砌地弄的，总之，上述做法目的为防潮。方砖墁地于卧室则冬季上置地屏，其构造乃用大约 3.5 厘米厚的木板，下置搁栅三根，四隅以四矮脚承之，宽为 100 厘米，长为 133 厘米，可自由移动。按房间大小安置，一般每间纵向块数按步架决定，即一步距离置地屏一块，横向则按面阔大小而定数之多寡，其高度约低于石鼓顶面 3 厘米。《长物志》所指"地屏则间可用之，……然总不如细砖之雅，南方卑湿，空铺最宜，略多费耳"，可以参证。至于用三和土瓦地，或在原地面加石灰夯实，不再铺砖，皆受经济条件之限制，故在披屋、厨房等为节省计亦用此法。另有灰土中加盐卤之法。李渔《一家言·居室部》载有以不规则粗砖铺成冰裂纹、肖龟纹的。在江南，砖铺地及夯土地面日久对防潮似起作用不大。一般居住房以木地板为最适用。

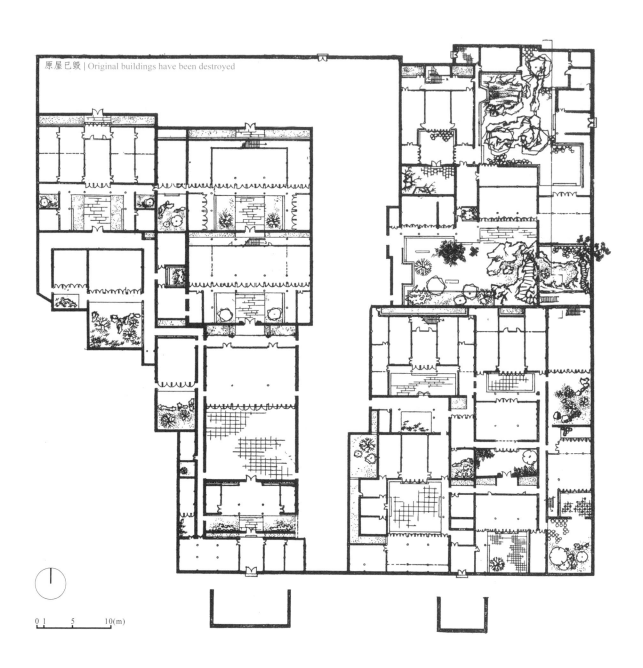

原屋已毁 | Original buildings have been destroyed

0 1   5   10(m)

0 1   5   10(m)

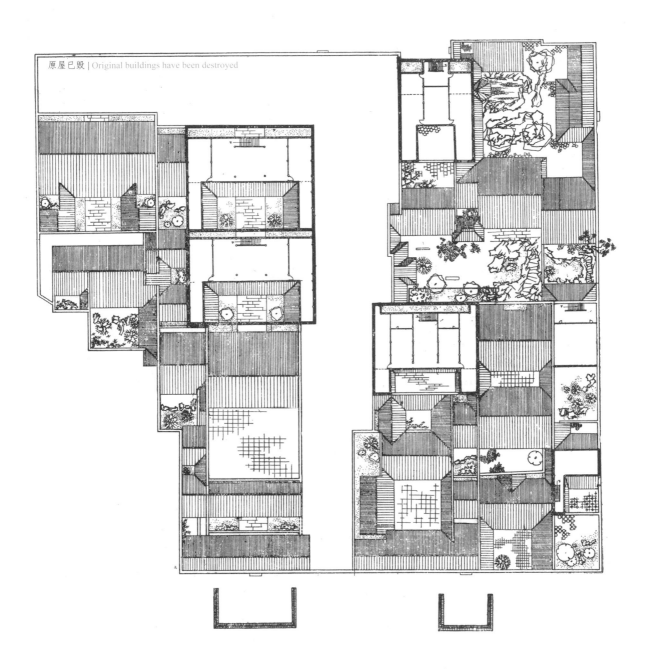

原屋已毁 | Original buildings have been destroyed

对页上：金太史场平斋一层平面图
对页下：金太史场平斋花厅剖面图
本页：金太史场平斋二层平面图

Opposite top: Ground floor plan of Pingzhai at Jintaishichang
Opposite bottom: Section of flower hall of Pingzhai at Jintaishichang
This page: First floor plan of Pingzhai at Jintaishichang

左上：醋库巷柴宅花厅白粉墙及石板铺地天井
右上：金太史场平斋照壁
下：剪金巷某宅天井绿化

Top left: Painted wall and courtyard covered with stone blocks of Chai's residence at Cuku Alley
Top right: Zhaobi of Pingzhai at Jintaishichang
Bottom: Plants at courtyard of a residence at Jianjin Alley

左上：天官坊陆宅砖砌墙
右上：宋仙洲巷张宅砖砌墙
下：宋仙洲巷张宅砖砌空斗墙

Top left: Wall with inlaid bricks of Lu's residence at Tianguan Fang

Top right: Wall with inlaid bricks of Zhang's residence at Songxianzhou Alley

Bottom: Hollow wall with inlaid bricks of Zhang's residence at Songxianzhou Alley

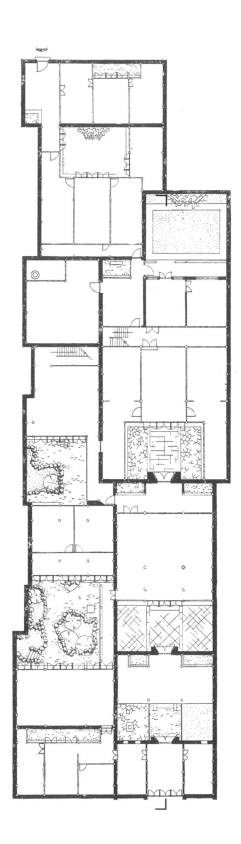

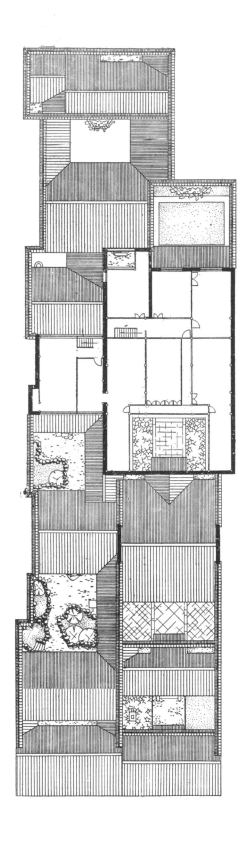

0 1 3 5(m)

对页左：宋仙洲巷张宅一层平面图
对页右：宋仙洲巷张宅二层平面图
本页：宋仙洲巷张宅剖面图

Opposite left: Ground floor plan of Zhang's residence at Songxianzhou Alley
Opposite right: First floor plan of Zhang's residence at Songxianzhou Alley
This page: Section of Zhang's residence at Songxianzhou Alley

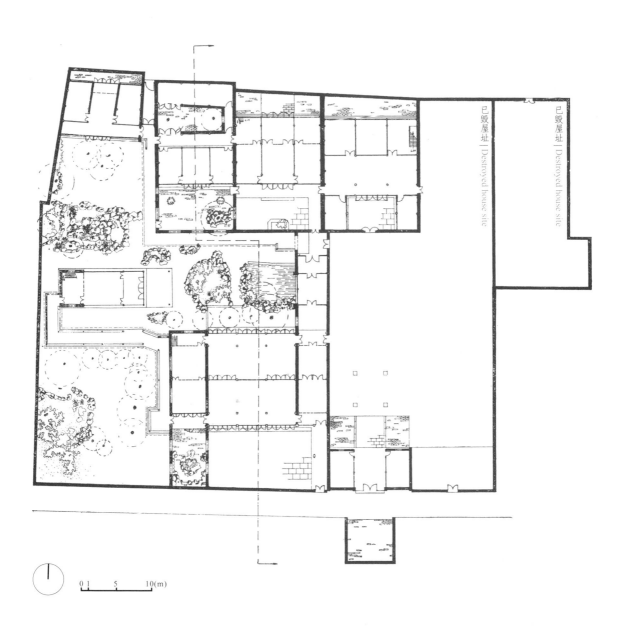

已毁屋址 | Destroyed house site
已毁屋址 | Destroyed house site

0 1   5   10(m)

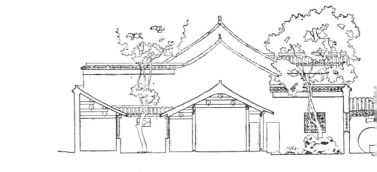

本页上：醋库巷柴宅一层平面图
对页上：醋库巷柴宅二层平面图
　下：醋库巷柴宅剖面图

This page top: Ground floor plan of Chai's residence at Cuku Alley
Opposite top: First floor plan of Chai's residence at Cuku Alley
Bottom: Section of Chai's residence at Cuku Alley

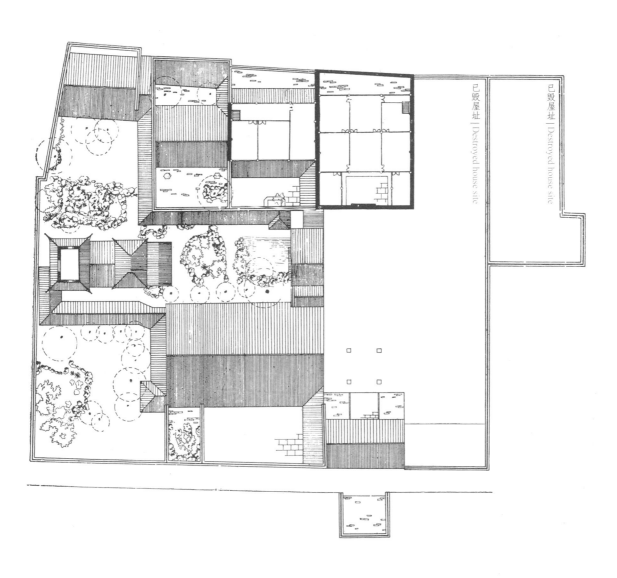

已毀屋址 | Destroyed house site

已毀屋址 | Destroyed house site

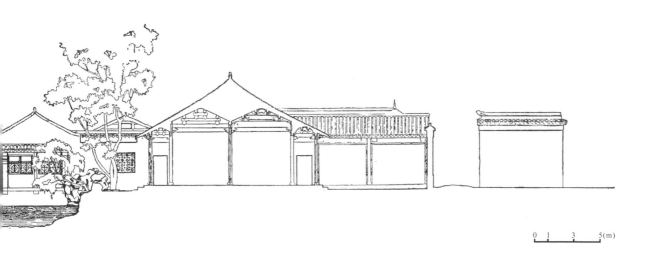

0 1 3 5(m)

柱与柱础　柱皆为直柱，柱下开十字槽以透气。若干明代建筑柱身皆有显著的卷杀，其法沿至清乾隆年间尚微具初态。柱形有圆柱、方柱，方柱有抹角与四角刻海棠曲线者。附近常熟环秀街环秀居（顾宅）花厅，其柱与础皆作瓣状，在苏州地区尚属仅见，想苏州过去定有此做法，惜今遗物无存。柱作长柱，其尺寸与一般住宅厅堂比例关系：如开间一市丈（约3.3 米）的，檐柱径八市寸（约 26.7厘米），金柱径视檐柱加二成。小型房屋柱径有用小头（柱的顶部）四市寸（约 13.3 厘米）者（直径为准）。

柱础有平础、木榰、木鼓、石鼓、石碇（苏南称"篮盆磉"）等类型，更有在覆盆上加木鼓的。大致用平础及木榰、木鼓的房屋皆为明构，古老相传"青石阶沿木鼓墩"为江南明构

Column and Column Base

The column used for support is always straight. A cross shaped groove is carved at the bottom for ventilation. Several houses of Ming dynasty have significant curving at the top of the column. This style of construction has been in effect until Qianlong period in Qing dynasty. The column can be either round or square shaped. The square shaped columns are curved at the edge, or have Haitang shaped curves carved at all four corners. The flower hall of Huanxiuju (Gu's residence) on Huanxiu Street in nearby Changshu has column and column base that are all shaped like pedals. This is the only place where this style can be found in Suzhou area. It is imaginable that this technique can be found at Suzhou once upon a time, unfortunately no remnant can be found today. The columns are long, and halls that have one Zhang (3.3 m) wide bays have eave columns with a diameter of eight Cun (26.7 cm). The diameter of a Jinzhu column may be twenty percent more than that of an eave column. The smaller house has top part with four-cun (13.3 cm) diameter.

The column base can be flat stone, wood chopping block, wood drum, stone drum or stone chopping block (Lanpensang style in Sunan area). There is also wood drum placed on top of a stone block. The flat stone, wood chopping block, or wood drum style supports are used in houses constructed during Ming dynasty. The ancient saying "black stone step, wood drum support" describes the characteristics of Ming construction in Jiangnan area, which is not groundless. Zhang's residence on Dongbei Street, Ding's residence at Daru Alley, and Gu's residence at Tieping Alley were all built during Ming period with the characteristics described above. The wood drum can be built in two fashions. The bottom part of column is first cut to a square. A round wood drum that is square in the middle then covers the square section of column. This is a fake drum construction, and the technique to accomplish this is simple. The other style is to place a wood drum outside a round column. The construction is similar to the aforementioned style. The Qixiang Gongsuo at Wenya Long (Wen Zhenmeng's residence during Ming dynasty) has column support constructed in the latter style. This also illustrates the style used to construct residences in Xiuning region of Anhui province during Ming dynasty This style was commonly used during Ming dynasty in Jiangnan region. The older small residences use a stone block instead of a stone drum for eave column support. This is because the stone block is slightly taller then stone drum, and provides a better moisture isolation. At the time of late Ming and early Qing dynasty, luxury residences use a plan Fupeng, or a Fupeng carved with lotus leave shape such as Yuanxiangtang in Zhuozheng Garden. There is also the placement of a wood drum on top of a Fupeng. This style is only found in Wenmiao Temple in Suzhou, but it is also used in houses of East Dongting Hill region. There is also relief carved on stone drum, or short stone column on top of stone drums that are used for support.

特征，是有根据的，如东北街张宅、大儒巷丁宅、铁瓶巷顾宅等之明构皆如是。木鼓做法有二：一种是柱从底部砍切作方形，外包以木鼓，为虚假性的，施工较易；另一种是将木鼓包在圆柱之外，其法与前者相同。文衙弄七襄公所（明文震孟宅）所见便是后一种，证以安徽休宁明代住宅所用者，其为明代江南通行做法。小型住宅较旧者，檐柱皆用石碛，因较石鼓为高，防潮效果略好。豪华住宅在明末清初者，有用素覆盆，或覆盆雕刻作荷叶状，如拙政园远香堂。更有于覆盆上加木鼓，在苏州虽仅于府文庙见到，但在洞庭东山民居中亦有之。此外，石鼓上施雕刻，或石鼓上连短石柱一段等形状，间有见到。

上：南石子街潘宅石鼓柱础
下左：东北街邮电大厅贴砖墙及柱础
下右：铁瓶巷顾宅明代木质柱础

Top: Stone-drum base of column of Pan's residence on Nanshizi Street
Bottom left: Brick-covered wall and stand post of the post office building on Dongbei Street
Bottom right: Wood base of column in Ming dynasty of Gu's residence at Tieping Alley

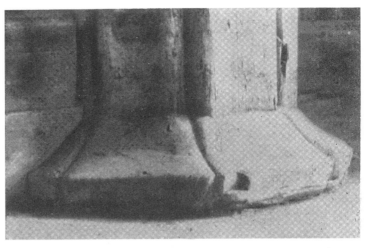

上：常熟市环秀街顾宅明代瓣形木质柱础
中：西百花巷太平天国某王府木质柱础
下：震泽县洞庭东山某宅木鼓柱础

Top: Petaled wood base of column in Ming dynasty of Gu's residence on Huanxiu
    Street, Changshu
Middle: Wood base of column of a Prince's Mansion at Xibaihua Alley
Bottom: Wood-drum base of column of a residence in East Dongting Hill, Zhenze

楼面 苏州旧住宅，一般来讲楼层作储藏之用为多，而若干大住宅以建高楼斗富，楼层遂有作居住之用。其做法于大柁上置龙骨（搁栅），其间距按檩数而定，大型楼房龙骨断面为方形，小型则为圆形。方形龙骨断面为 11 厘米 ×18 厘米，大柁约比龙骨高三倍。圆形龙骨乃将直径约 14 厘米圆木上下砍去约 3 厘米。楼板厚度最大者达 4 厘米，小者亦有 2.8 厘米，更有楼板之上铺方砖者与楼板上铺活动地屏者。地屏高度依门槛略低，如门槛高 23 厘米，地屏则高为 20 厘米。《一家言·居室部》谓："有用板作地者，又病其步履有声。"因此，楼面结构不得不用以上两法，此种做法过于浪费，究属少数。因为苏州夏季炎热，即使楼上亦置落地长窗。扶梯有设于厅后或两厢，早期亦有在避弄中者，如葑门彭宅、大儒巷潘宅。

Upper Story

The upper story of the traditional residences is mostly used for storage. Some large residences are built with upper levels to compete in luxury, but they also serve as living quarters. The construction involves placing joists on the girders. The number of purlin determines the distance between joists. The joist for large buildings has a square cross section, and the smaller houses use a round shaped joist. The square-shaped joists are approximately 11 cm by 18 cm in size, and girders are three times taller then joists. The round joists used in smaller houses are made by cutting three centimeters from both the top and bottom of a 14 cm diameter lumber. The thickness of floorboard can vary form 2.8 cm to 4 cm. Square tiles or movable floor screen can even be placed on these floorboards. The height of floor screen is slightly lower than the threshold of door. For example if the threshold is 23 cm high, then the floor screen is 20 cm. It is stated in the Chapter of Residences of *Yijiayan*, "boards are used to make floors, but walking on it produces a great amount of noises." This means that floors for upper stories have to be made with either a floor screen, or tile which is very expensive to make. Long lattice windows are used for upper story due to the warm summers. The staircases are placed behind the main hall or at the side. There is also staircase placed at Bilong, which is typical in early constructions such as Peng's residence at Gate Feng, and Pan's residence at Daru Alley.

景德路杨宅楼层

Upper story of Yang's residence on Jingde Road

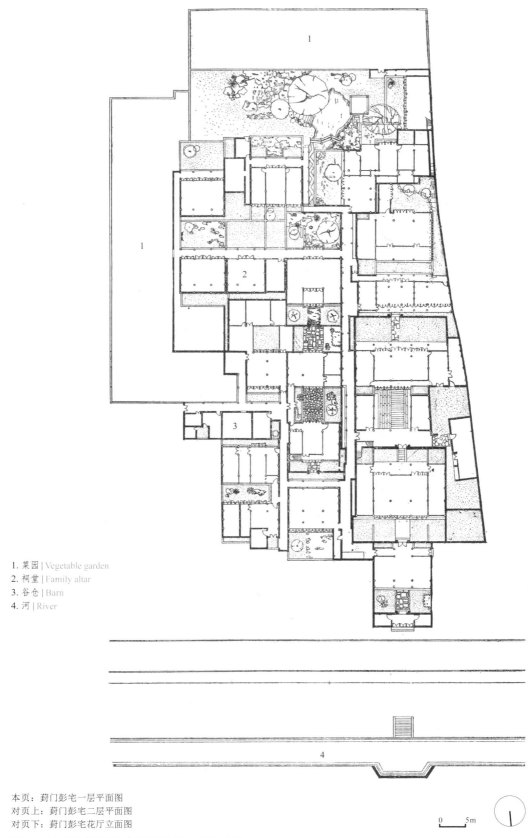

1. 菜园 | Vegetable garden
2. 祠堂 | Family altar
3. 谷仓 | Barn
4. 河 | River

0   5m

本页：莘门彭宅一层平面图
对页上：莘门彭宅二层平面图
对页下：莘门彭宅花厅立面图

This page: Ground floor plan of Peng's residence at Gate Feng
Opposite top: First floor plan of Peng's residence at Gate Feng
Opposite bottom: Elevation of flower hall of Peng's residence at Gate Feng

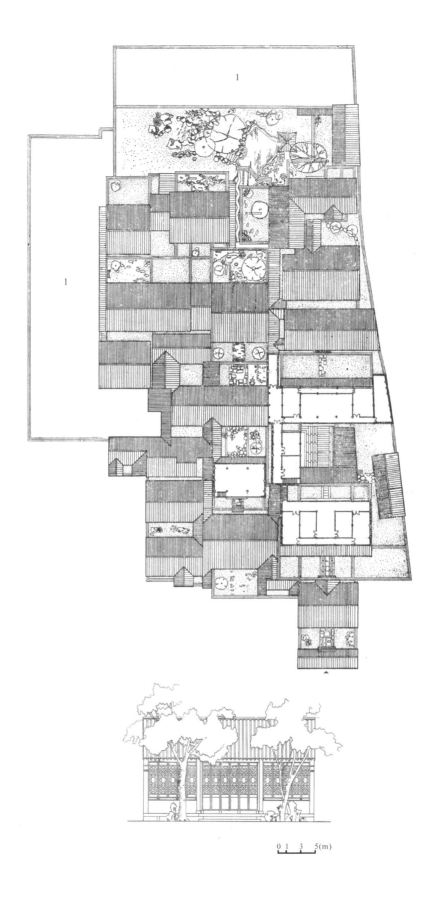

1

1

0 1 3 5(m)

梁架 苏州旧住宅的梁架结构在中国古建筑中是变化较多的。除正规木架外，充分利用草架。在形式方面可分为两类：（一）彻上露明造，大部分为一般小型建筑；（二）用草架施覆水椽及翻轩（卷棚）的。彻上露明造的小型房屋，大部分用圆料直材，山面多用穿斗式，明间缝用五架梁式，如为厅堂，各缝梁架则均砍杀作月梁形。铁瓶巷顾宅轿厅（明代），梁架用小五架梁，将后柱易为长柱，便于装门，与《园冶》所示相同。此建筑与东北街李宅清康熙六十年（1721年）所建大厅，前后不施翻轩，中安七架梁者，皆为苏州住宅中所罕见。

草架一端，计成《园冶》云："草架乃厅堂之必用者，凡屋添卷（翻轩）用天沟，且费事不耐久，故以草架表里整齐。"又云："重椽，草架上椽也，乃屋中假屋也。凡屋隔分不仰顶，用重椽覆水可观。惟廊构连屋，或构倚墙一披而下，断不可少斯。"据此应用草架的理由甚明白。但更主要者，实由于江南夏季炎热，施覆水椽可隔

Roof Frame The structure of traditional residence roof frame of Suzhou is one of the most flexible among all traditional Chinese architecture designs. It makes use of the rough frame (an unexposed frame) to its fullest extent in addition to the regular wood frame. The style of roof frame can be devided into two categories. The first style is a completely exposed frame and there is no rough frame. This style is most commonly seen for small structures. The second is using rough frame with Fushuichuan (oblique rafters) and arched ceilings. The first style of buildings most utilize straight and round lumber and the side of the building uses Chuandou (means piercing brace, i.e. the columns of building passing beyond the braces) style brace. Central bay of the building in small residence is constructed with a five-purlin-beam system (Wujialiang). When a hall is built, each of the beams is cut to a crescent shape. The carriage hall of Gu's residence at Tieping Alley Gu residence was built during Ming dynasty. This structure used a miniature five-purlin-beam system (Xiaowujialiang), and converted the rear column into a long column so it is easier to install doors. The book *Yuanye*(《园冶》) noted this style of construction. Main hall of Li's residence on Dongbei Street was built during 1721 (60th year of Kangxi period during Qing dynasty) do not have arched ceilings and has a seven-purlin-beam system in the center. Both the carriage hall of Gu's residence and main hall of Li's residence are rarities in Suzhou residence construction techniques.

Ji Cheng wrote in *Yuanye*, "Rough frame is a necessity for halls. It is very cumbersome to add arched ceiling like Tiangou structure. The arched ceiling built by adopting this technique is not able to maintain long. So rough frame is the preferred method of construction as it also gives a very clean view." It then notes, "Chongchuan is the rafter on top of rough frame, it is the house inside a house. Chongchuan with oblique rafters can make a house without depressing the top presentable. It is a necessity to use Chongchuan for passages that are connected to the house, or any structure that relies on the wall as a single structure." This clearly shows the reason of building a rough frame. It is more important to understand that during summer this region of China can be rather hot, and oblique rafters in construction can help shield the heat, and prevent the severe cold, making its style and function an intertwined necessity. Oblique rafter is also very important because it is easy to divide the building into sections, and makes inside ceiling of the building presentable.

The roof frame structure of a hall in traditional Suzhou residence follows the rough frame and seven-purlin-beam system shown in *Yuanye*. The book *Yuanye* says, "The so called five-purlin beam is the passing beam in the middle of a hall. If there is another section added in on each side, then it becomes a seven-purlin-beam frame. If a section of arched ceiling is added in front, then it is necessary to use rough frames to raise the ceiling. The lack of a rough frame will cause the front eave to drop low, making the building interior dark. The addition of a corridor in front will open up the area further." This passage shows that five-purlin-beam system is most frequently adopted. There can either be one or two sections (Juan) of arched ceiling added to the front of a building. The outer section of arched ceiling of some buildings that add two sections in front is converted to use oblique rafter and is constructed as a passage corridor such as the hall of Zhang's residence on Dongbei Street. The addition of multiple sections of arched ceiling on a hall type building makes its floor plan further like a long rectangle. Roof structure for flower hall and study is especially flexible. Both round and rectangular shaped lumbers are used to maximize the variations of rough frame design. For example the Yuanyang (companion) hall would use rectangular shaped lumber on one side, and round lumber on the other with the same six-purlin-beam system. Both sides will have arched ceiling with rough frame built

热兼可防寒，其形式与功能是相结合的，至于便于分隔、仰观屋顶表里整齐亦重要因素。

苏州旧住宅厅堂梁架结构一般是与《园冶》所示草架式及七架列式相同。《园冶》所谓："五架梁，乃厅堂中过梁也。如前后各添一架，合七架梁列架式；如前添卷，必须草架而轩敞，不然前檐深下，内黑暗者，斯故也。如欲宽展，前再添一廊。"因此，厅堂是以四界大梁（五架梁）为主，前施翻轩（卷棚），其数有一卷或二卷的，更有前用二卷，而其外一卷改用覆水椽作廊式者，如东北街张宅大厅。厅堂卷数加多，则其平面呈纵长方形。花厅梁架与书斋梁架结构变化尤多，材料亦扁圆兼用，极尽草架变化之能事。如鸳鸯厅，南北两面，一用五界回顶（六架梁）"扁作"，一用五界回顶（六架梁）"圆料"，皆作卷棚式，上施草架式。有前后各施卷棚二卷、上构草架者，如东北街张宅花厅（即拙政园三十六鸳鸯馆）。而阊门叶家弄倪宅（原为叶天池旧宅）

书斋屋顶用大弧形卷棚，若船篷上施草架，简洁明快，实为佳例。至于厅内减去平柱而易为花篮（垂莲）柱，苏南称为"花篮厅"，其做法：花篮（垂莲）柱以三间通长整料贯之，其上檩条亦通长整料，故一般面阔较小，受材料限制，如东北街李宅鸳鸯厅、修仙巷宋宅花篮厅。楼厅用翻轩（卷棚），底层在腰檐之下，称"副檐轩"。如无腰檐，亦有于金柱与廊檐柱间施之，称"楼下轩"。或有腰檐作骑廊轩，则轩仅一半于檐下。并有在楼层平座下加小翻轩，楼层屋顶檐口下间有用之。史家巷彭宅楼鸳鸯厅做法，南北皆列翻轩，以覆水椽形成双层屋顶。至于翻轩名称，系根据弯椽形状而定，因椽之形式不同，可分船篷轩、鹤颈轩、菱角轩、海棠轩、一枝香轩、方形轩、茶壶档轩等。翻轩根据不同构造有：抬头轩、磕头轩、半磕头轩等。据位置不同则有廊轩与内轩之别。

柱之长度与围径视开间而定，梁之长度视进深而定。扁作大梁如高一市尺八市寸（约 60 厘米），机面为

on top. There are also the cases that two sections of arched ceiling will be added to both front and rear of the building with rough frame built on top. This is the case of flower hall of Zhang's residence on Dongbei Street, which is also known as the Thirty-Six Pairs of Mandarin Ducks Hall of Zhuozheng Garden. Ni's residence at Yejia Long near Gate Chang (old residence of Ye Tianchi) has a study with a two-section rooftop of large curve shaped arched ceiling which looks like a boat roof. Rough frame is placed on top of arched ceiling in the study at Ni 's residence at Yejia Long making the interior view clean and simple. This study at Ni's residence is a perfect example of this type of structure. The Hualan (flower basket) hall is where the Hualan (also known as hanging lotus) column is used instead of the Ping column. This is constructed by having a single piece of lumber that is three bays wide to support the columns. The purlin above is also made from a single piece of lumber. This requirement limits the width of the building. The companion hall of I i's residence on Dongbei Street, and the flower basket hall of Song's residence at Xiuxian Alley are both constructed in this fashion. The two-story building that has the bottom of arched ceiling below the waist eave is called a waist-eave arched ceiling. There is also the Louxiaxuan, which is a building with no waist eave, and the arched ceiling is built between the Jinzhu column and corridor eave column. The other style of arched ceiling, Qilangxuan, is constructed with half of the arched ceiling below the waist eave. Small arched ceiling structure can also be built below the falt base of the upper floor, or below the roof eave of a building. The companion hall of Peng's residence at Shijia Alley is built with arched ceiling both on the north and the south side of the structure. There is a double ceiling constructed with oblique rafters in this structure. The arched ceiling can be named based on the shape of the curved rafter: perched head, kowtow, or half kowtow. There is also arched ceiling for the corridor, and arched ceiling for building interior. There are different shapes of rafter including boat roof, crane neck, Lingjiao, Haitang, incense, square, teapot etc.

The height and diameter of a column is based on the width of the room. Beam length is based on the depth of the room. If the rectangular beam is one Chi and eight Cun tall, then the top is one Chi wide, and the bottom is eight Cun wide. The top is wide, while the lower part is narrow. This compensates a perspective vision when looking from below. Such structure is more advanced than the architecture in southern Jiangsu province. The beams are all shaped like crescent, and the beams in early Qing constructions have a tall and graceful outline. The slopes of the beam are low, and the carvings on the beam are neat and soft. This style of beams follows the style used during Ming dynasty. The lumber used during Qianlong and Jiaqing period of Qing dynasty is very strong and thick. The cuts and carvings on the lumber are orderly. After the Tongguang period (Tongzhi and Guangxu periods, abbriviated as Tongguang) the lumber became relatively light, and the carvings are relaxed and flat. This is strongly correlated with the economic situation, and the techniques used in handicrafts at that time. The wood inserts below the beam end, and the mountain, fog and cloud carvings below the ridge truss are the most visible carvings. Wood inserts used during early Qing constructions have a slightly round outline, and the carving is very neat and exquisite. The style closely follows those built during Ming dynasty. Carvings on wood inserts are deep during Qianlong and Jiaqing period, and those in more recent buildings are flat but more complex. Comparing some buildings with ascertained time, the ratio of four-section (five-purlin) beam cross-section based on buildings is as follows. The late Ming and early Qing construction such as Shiluntang at Qixiang Gongshuo has a height-width ratio of three to two. This ratio changed to two to one for buildings such as Anrentang of Jin's residence at Bifeng Fang and the Qingyintang of Lu's residence at Tianguan Fang, which were all built during Qianlong and Jiaqing period. The two to one ratio was followed

一市尺（约 33.3 厘米），底面为八市寸（约 26.6 厘米），上宽下狭，其原因乃由下向上望，不致因视差而变形，此一般言苏南建筑者未及之。梁架作皆为月梁，早期的轮廓挺秀，斜项平缓，雕刻工整柔和，犹存晚明规。清乾嘉时，用材硕健，砍杀雕刻规正。同光以后，用材较轻巧，雕刻松弛扁平，此乃与当时经济背景与手工艺作风密切相关。梁头下之插木，脊桁下之山雾云，为雕刻最突出之处。早期插木轮廓四周带圆形，雕刻工整，剔透玲珑，与明代颇相近。乾嘉时期，雕刻厚重，其后之作，雕刻繁缛扁平。四界梁（五架梁）断面比例，从几处年代较准确之建筑作比较，明末清初，其高与宽之比例为 3:2（七襄公所世纶堂）；乾嘉时期，其高与宽比例为 2:1（碧凤坊金宅安仁堂、天官坊陆宅清荫堂）；同光以后，其高与宽之比仍因之。其实材料本身还是近 3:2 之断面，不过在梁上两侧覆加辅材二条，形成较高之假断面，唯于受压点，以块木填实。从嘉庆以后，梁上断面逐渐开始趋向上大下小，此式直至晚清民初后成为香山匠师所遵准绳。

　　早期梁架因断面低，故在山界梁（三架梁）下于斗上置矮柱承托，脊桁下亦然，致使屋面坡度较平缓，其后，梁架断面增高，矮柱亦可略去。凡豪华之梁架，在斗下加荷叶墩，又有梁架施彩绘者，前者如大儒巷潘宅，后者如古市巷吴宅、东北街今邮局等，皆乾隆时厅堂。小型建筑，其梁架以"圆作"为多。牌科（斗拱）卷杀，早期者在瓣的两面不凹内，乾隆时的建筑已开始有萌芽，此端与梁柱砍杀同为苏南建筑考订年代之特征。早期厅堂前后不用翻轩，廊用单步弯梁，苏南称为"眉川"。早期断面狭而高，如东北街李宅大厅、拙政园乾隆年间建远香堂。而富郎中巷陈宅之眉川过于繁缛，已非苏南常态，似受宁波建筑之影响。

after Tongguang period. In reality the cross section of lumber is still closer to a three to two ratio, but there are two supplemental pieces that was added to both sides of the beam to form the higher false cross section. The pressure points are filled with wood chunks. The cross section of beams built after the Jiaqing period start to follow the shape of an inverted trapezoid. This style was followed as the standard for builders from Xiangshan region until late Qing and the early Republican period.

　　The early roof frames have a low cross section, thus a short beam is placed above the Dou (brace) at the hill section (three-purlin) beam as well as below the ridge truss. This reduces the slope of the roof. The increase in cross section of roof frame allowed the short beam to be omitted. The more luxurious roof frames have a lotus leave shaped stand below the Dou. There is also roof frame that is painted in color. The former can be found at Pan's residence at Daru Alley. The latter is evident at both Wu's residence at Gushi Alley and the post office building on Dongbei Street. These structures were all constructed during Qianlong period. Most of the smaller residences construct roof frames with round lumber. The cut of Paike (Dougong or braces) during early constructions is done on the side of the pedals and does not concave in. This started during the Qianlong period. This along with the cut of beam and column are important characteristics in identifying the year of construction for south Jiangsu region structures. The early halls did not use arched ceiling in the front or rear. The single curved beam used for corridors is called Meichuan in this region. Early constructions have cross-sections that are narrow but tall such as the main hall of Li's residence on Dongbei Street, and the Yuanxiangtang of Zhuozheng Garden built during Qianlong period. Chen's residence of Fulangzhong Alley has an extremely elaborate Meichuan, which is not commonly seen in this region. There seem to be some influence from Ningbo region on the design of this structure.

修仙巷宋宅花篮厅梁架及翻轩

Roof frame and arched ceiling of flower basket hall of Song's residence
at Xiuxian Alley

0   1   2   3(m)

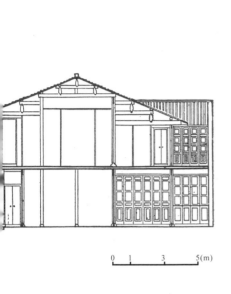

0 1 3 5(m)

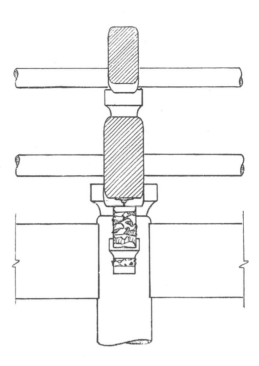

0 10 20 30(cm)

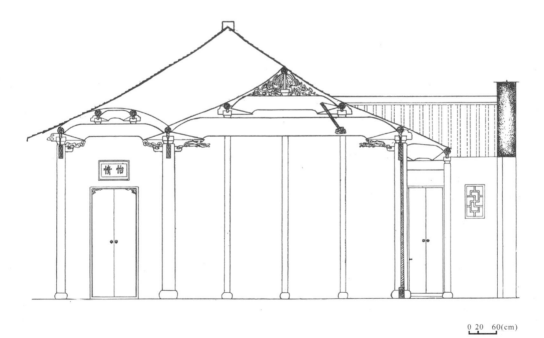

怡情

0 20 60(cm)

对页上：碧凤坊金宅剖面图
对页下：碧凤坊金宅花园剖面图
本页上：碧凤坊金宅大厅明间梁架剖面图
本页下：碧凤坊金宅大厅剖面图

Opposite top: Section of Jin's residence at Bifeng Fang

Opposite bottom: Section of garden of Jin's residence at Bifeng Fang

This page top: Section of roof frame of main hall of Jin's residence at Bifeng Fang

This page bottom: Section of main hall of Jin's residence at Bifeng Fang

上：文衙弄旧文宅（艺圃）世纶堂梁架
下：卫道观前潘宅大厅梁架

Top: Roof frame of Shiluntang of Wen's residence at Wenya Long
Bottom: Roof frame of main hall of Pan's residence at Weidaoguanqian

楼厅梁架模型

Model of roof frame of storied hall

上：鸳鸯厅模型
下：鸳鸯厅模型正立面

Top: Model of companion hall
Bottom: Front of the model of companion hall

上：鸳鸯厅梁架模型俯视
下：鸳鸯厅模型侧面

Top: Over look of roof frame of companion hall
Bottom: Side view of the model of companion hall

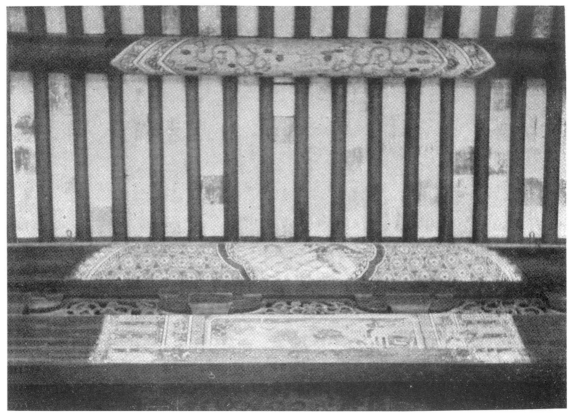

上：东北街太平天国忠王府正殿彩绘
下：东北街某宅大厅彩画梁架

Top: Colored painting of main hall of Prince Zhong's Mansion
Bottom: Roof frame with colored drawing of a residence on Dongbei Street

上：东北街李宅海棠轩
下：东北街某宅翻轩

Top: Haitang arched ceiling of Li's residence on Dongbei Street
Bottom: Arched ceiling of a residence on Dongbei Street

上：西百花巷程宅鹤颈轩
下：文衙弄旧文宅（艺圃）世纶堂梁架

Top: Crane-neck arched ceiling of Cheng's residence at Xibaihua Alley
Bottom: Roof frame of Shiluntang of Wen's residence at Wenya Long

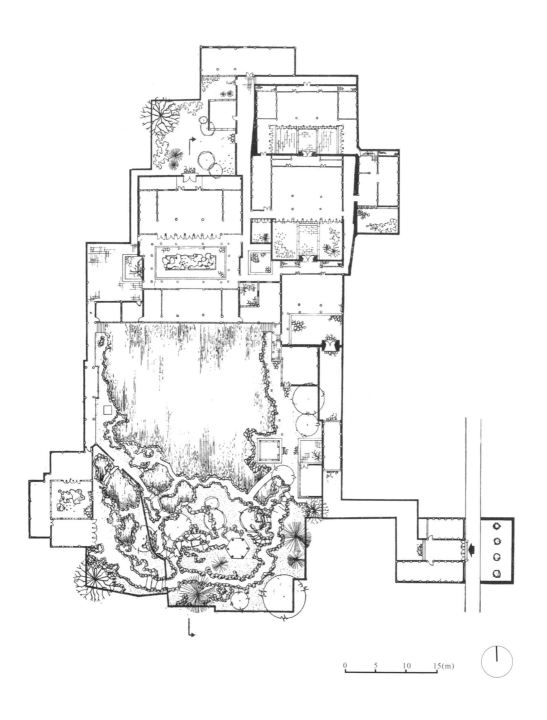

0 5 10 15(m)

0 1 3 5(m)

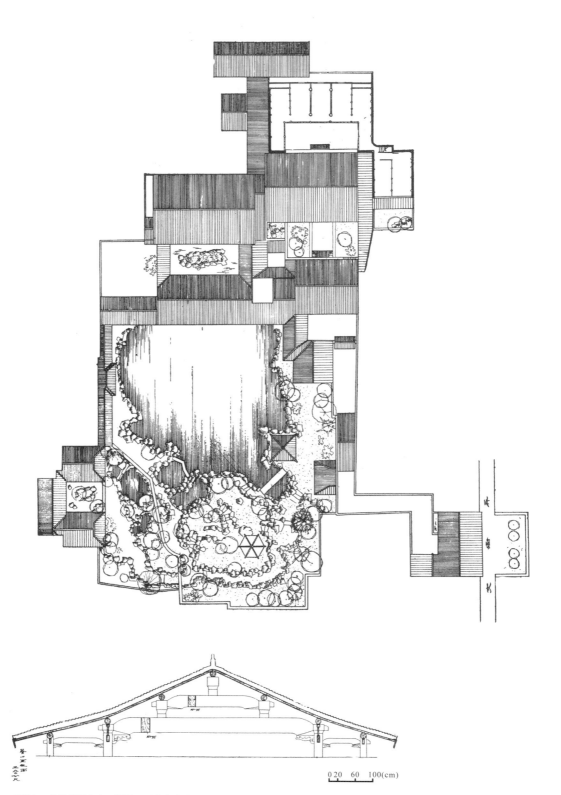

0 20 60   100(cm)

对页上：文衙弄旧文宅（艺圃）一层平面图
对页下：文衙弄旧文宅（艺圃）花园剖面图
本页上：文衙弄旧文宅（艺圃）二层平面图
本页下：文衙弄旧文宅（艺圃）世纶堂明间梁架图

Opposite top: Ground floor plan of Wen's residence at Wenya Long

Opposite bottom: Section of garden of Wen's residence at Wenya Long

This page top: First floor plan of of Wen's residence at Wenya Long

This page bottom: Section of roof frame of Shiluntang's central bay of Wen's residence at Wenya Long

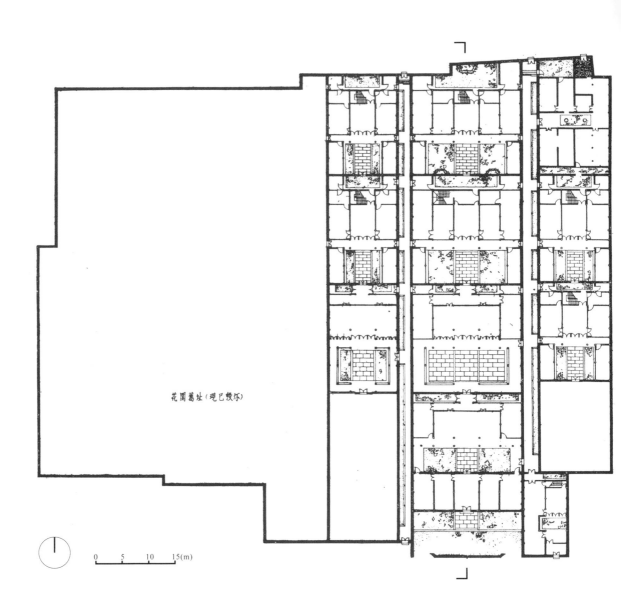

花园旧址（现已毁坏）

0　5　10　15(m)

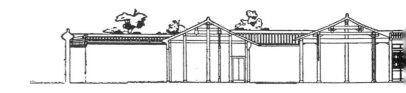

本页上：富郎中巷陈宅一层平面图
对页上：富郎中巷陈宅二层平面图
下：富郎中巷陈宅剖面图

This page top: Ground floor plan of Chen's residence at Fulangzhong Alley
Opposite top: First floor plan of Chen's residence at Fulangzhong Alley
Bottom: Section of Chen's residence at Fulangzhong Alley

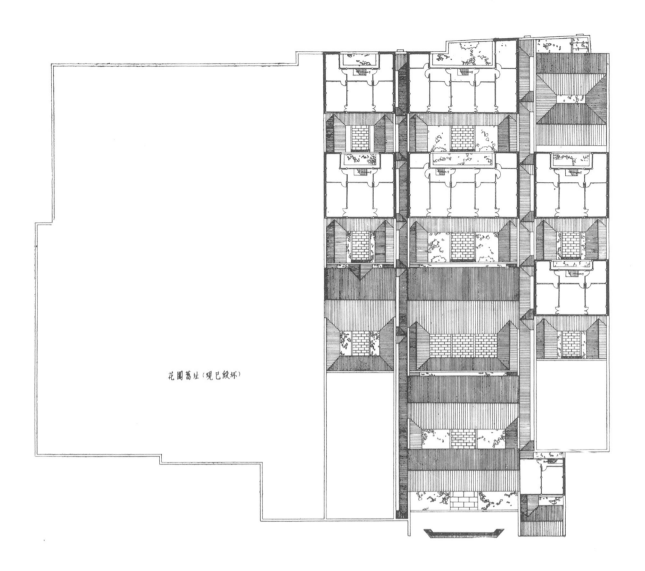

花园旧址（现已毁坏）

0 1 3 5(m)

屋面 苏州旧住宅之屋顶以硬山式为主，屋脊按形式有"雉毛""纹头""甘蔗""哺鸡"等名称，亦有不用脊者。花厅有歇山式，如不用脊亦有之。瓦用蝴蝶瓦，压七露三，其下铺望砖，近檐口部分以石灰加固。瓦头施花边、滴水。间有少数用望板，更有用篾箔者，而简陋房屋则不用望板直接由椽承瓦。屋之坡度乾隆后趋向高陡。一般厅堂檐皆出飞椽。楼厅腰檐出飞椽，上檐飞椽往往略去。花厅如用四落水屋顶，其屋角起翘，有老戗发戗、嫩戗发戗、水戗发戗等。

戗的形式一般用"朝板戗"，因其形如古时上朝之笏板而得名。稍事装饰者，戗上加刻花纹如杨叶般，称"杨叶戗"。其他亦有饰梅花枝，均为踵事增华罢了。

Roof

The gable style roof is most widely seen in traditional Suzhou houses. The roof ridge can be categorized by pattern into Zhimao, Wentou, Ganzhe, Buji etc. There are also some that do not have a ridge. Flush and gable style roof can be found in flower hall, but there is also the ridgeless style. The tiles are convex and concave tiles laid with seventy percent overlap. Wangzhuan is a flat thin brick and placed beneath the tiles. Lime mixture is used to secure the tiles along eaves. The end tiles have decorative pieces, and roof gutters. There is also use of wood boards and bamboo sheets in place of Wangzhuan. The simpler, low cost house has tiles directly laid onto the roof frame. The slope of roof increased after Qianlong period. There is flying rafters for most halls. The waist eaves of two story structures have flying rafters, and often the roof flying rafters are removed in this case. The pyramid style roof used with flower hall would have curved up along the four corners, and have styles like Laoqiangfaqiang (老戗发戗), Nenqiangfaqiang (嫩戗发戗), and Shuiqiangfaqiang (水戗发戗) etc.

The most commonly used style of Qiang is Chaobanqiang (朝板戗). This style of Qiang is similar in the shape of boards held by ministers (笏板) when emperor held court. The Qiang can be decorated with leaf, or flower patterns. Then the style is named after the type of pattern carved. These patterns and decorations are for the purpose of style.

嫩戗发戗模型

水戗发戗模型
Model of Shuiqiangfaqiang

老戗发戗模型

Model of Laoqiangfaqiang

间隔　苏州旧住宅之间隔甚为灵活，其大致可分四种：（一）薄砖墙，用于固定之分隔处，与建筑物垂直纵向为多。（二）屏门，平时作间隔用，可自由关启，又可卸下扩大空间。屏门有一面装木板，或两面皆装木板，后者属于豪华住宅。明代及清初之屏门犹沿袭明代做法，门枋用圆木，门之宽度较大，如马大箓巷邱宅残存者。最豪华的厅堂中甚至有用整块银杏木制成，如西百花巷程宅、东北街张宅。张宅曾为太平天国忠王府，原髹朱漆，其痕迹尚存。一般皆刷白色。（三）纱槅，即固定槅扇用来做间隔，其裙板上雕花，槅心（苏南称"心仔"）易用银杏木施雕，皆法书名画或博古等，填以石绿，古色成趣，或裱糊名

Partitions

Partitions in traditional Suzhou residences are very flexible. They can be categorized into the following four categories. The first category is thin brick wall. It is used for fixed partitions. This type of partition is built along the depth of the building. The second category consists of screen doors. This is a temporary separator that can be opened freely, and can be removed completely to increase total space. Screen door can be formed with either one or two wood panels. The latter form is more commonly found in luxurious houses. Screen doors of late Ming and early Qing dynasty are built in the same fashion as those built during mid Ming dynasty. The screen frame uses round wood and are relatively wide. The remnant door at Qiu's residence at Madalu Alley is an outstanding example. There are also screen doors that are built with one full piece of gingko wood in some very luxurious halls as those built in Cheng's residence at Xibaihua Alley, and Zhang's residence on Dongbei Street. Zhang's residence was at one time Prince Zhong's Mansion of Taiping Tianguo (太平天国忠王府 , Taiping Tianguo is a peasent uprising that occurred during Qing dynasty). It was painted red, and traces of red paint can still be seen on the screen doors. Screen doors are usually painted white in residences. The third category is Shage, or fixed screens. This type have relieves carved on the skirt board (Qunban written as 裙板). The central part (pronounced as Gexin or

Xinzai in south Jiangsu province) of a fixed screen is made of gingko for carving easily. The carvings include famous calligraphy and paintings. Green color is filled into the crevices to make it look classic. It can also be pasted with calligraphy or paintings of famous people, or relieves from stone carvings, even fixed with a light cloth. These give the screen doors an elegant look. The fixed screen at Xi's residence at Sanyuan Fang use Zitanmu and Hongmu. There are some screens made from Hongmu and Nanmu （Zitanmu 紫檀木, Nanmu 楠木 and Hongmu 红木 are types of hardwood that are commonly used to build furniture and construct buildings) that was moved from old residences to Liuyuan Garden and Suzhou Museum. The most frequently seen material of fixed screens from large residences is made of gingko. The forth category consists of flying panels which are the most flexible and fancy. The types of flying panels in Suzhou are not as diverse as those in Beijing, but they are much more exquisite. The most often seen patterns on these flying panels are random lines, willow, circle with octagon. The panels are made out of gingko, with some Hongmu and Hualimu. If the two ends reach floor then they are called Luodizhao （落 地 罩 known as floor reaching panels). If the shape looks like a drape, and the two ends do not hang as low as the flying panels, it is called flying panel drapes. Drapes are placed between two columns and have either the swastika or vine patterns.

人字画及拓本等，有钉以轻纱的，亦颇雅洁。纱槅中，如三元坊席宅，用紫檀木及红木制，留园及苏州博物馆，有从旧民居中移来亦系红木、楠木制的。在大住宅中尤以银杏木制者为最普遍。（四）挂落飞罩，为房间中一种最灵活与巧妙的间隔。苏州旧住宅中的罩，种类虽不及北京之多，然玲珑轻巧则远在北京之上。其最常用者为乱纹飞罩、藤茎飞罩、圆方八角飞罩等，材料一般皆为银杏木，间有用红木与花梨木者。若两端及地，称为"落地罩"。如其形似挂落、两端下垂较飞罩为短，称为"飞罩挂落"。挂落则悬装于廊柱间枋子之间，以万字纹反复相连为多，亦有用藤茎的。

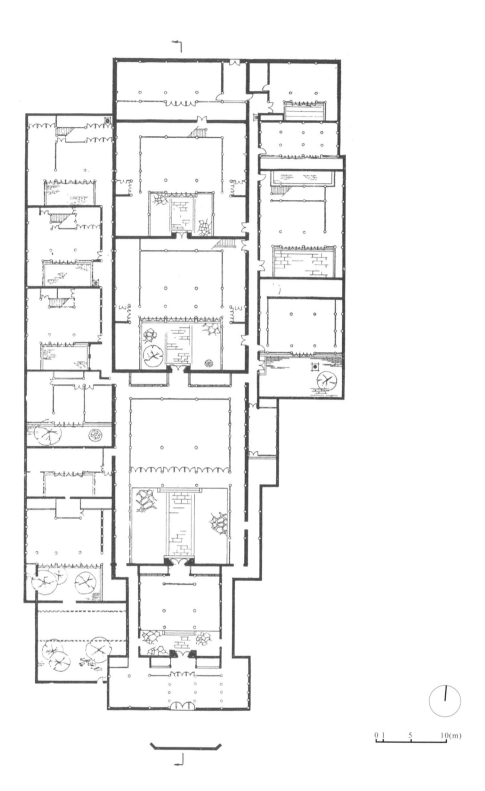

本页上：马大篾巷邱宅一层平面图
对页上：马大篾巷邱宅二层平面图
下：马大篾巷邱宅剖面图

This page top: Ground floor plan of Qiu's residence at Madalu Alley
Opposite top: First floor plan of Qiu's residence at Madalu Alley
Bottom: Section of Qiu's residence at Madalu Alley

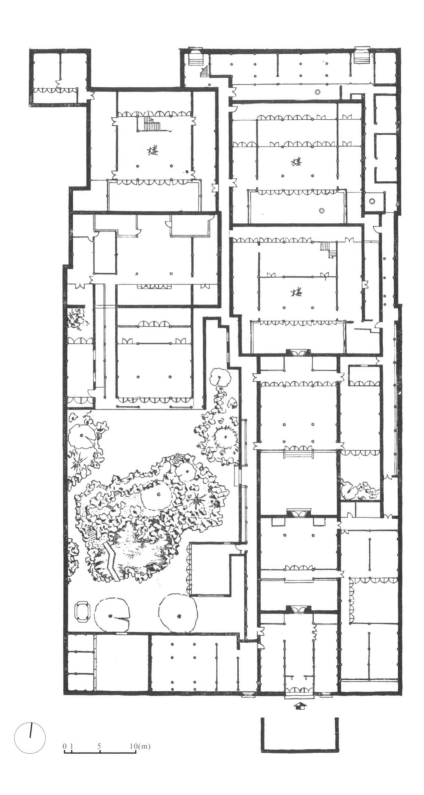

楼

楼

楼

0 1   5   10(m)

西百花巷程宅一层平面图

Ground floor plan of Cheng's residence at Xibaihua Alley

西百花巷程宅装修

Decoration of Cheng's residence at Xibaihua Alley

上：西百花巷程宅挂落
下：西百花巷程宅楼厅二层平座

Top: Flying panel drapes of Cheng's residence at Xibaihua Alley
Bottom: Flat base of the first floor of Cheng's residence at Xibaihua Alley

西百花巷程宅楼厅槅扇（门）

Lattices doors of storied hall of Cheng's residence at Xibaihua Alley

装折（装修）　苏州之装折为门窗、栏杆、挂落等之统称，即北方之内檐装修。窗有长窗、风窗、地坪窗、半窗、横风窗、和合窗、纱槅窗等。兹就习见于常例者分述于下。和合窗（支摘窗）一般上下三窗，但有上两窗做支窗，而其下一扇则改成两扇直立小窗，有所变化，如东北街张宅。又有外观做成直的地坪窗（槛窗）形，而实为和合窗的，如铁瓶巷任宅。横风窗有加于地坪窗之上下，形成一竖二横的构图。至于长窗，其形式如以时代而论，早期在心仔部分用柳条式、人字变六方式、柳条变井字式、井字变杂花式、玉砖街式、八方式、正斜方块、正斜万字、冰裂纹、网纹等，即都用横直棱条拼成，朴素无华，宜于贴纸或外配明瓦，间有用活动板者。此种图案犹明计成《园冶》所示之遗绪。后期则以宫式、葵式、回纹万字、如意凌（菱）花、海堂凌（菱）角等为多，更有插角乱纹嵌玻璃、冰纹嵌

Decoration

The decoration of building in Suzhou includes door, window, railing, and drapes. This is also called inner eave decoration in north China. The various types of windows used include long window, air window, floor window (地 坪 窗 pronounced as Dipingchuang), half window, horizontal air window, awning window, and fixed screen window. We will discuss some of the most commonly used styles. The awning windows are usually composed of three pieces stacked vertically. There is a type of variation where the bottom pane is converted to two small vertical windows such as the windows used in Zhang's residence on Dongbei Street. There is also a variation that the exterior is made to look like vertical floor window, but is actually a awning window such as Ren's residence at Tieping Alley. Horizontal air window can be placed above and below floor window to form a structure of one vertical and two horizontal. The long window or lattice doors have various shapes at different time. The patterns on the central part of the screens can be willow, " 人 " morphed into a six-sided shape, willow morphed into a " 井 " shape, " 井 " morphed into flower pattern, jade brick tile, octagon, various rectangle, Buddhist swastika shape, ice break pattern, fish net pattern etc. All of these patterns are formed with thin wood strips. The patterns are simplistic and clean. Paper or clear tiles can be attached to the patterns easily. There are also some that use moving boards. These patterns descend from those described in Ji Cheng's *Yuanye*. In the later periods, shapes such as Gong, sunflower, Buddhist swastika, S-shaped with rhombus, or crabapple with rhombus are used more frequently. There are also random line pattern, ice break pattern, sunflower pattern, flower knot pattern, or octagon pattern that have glass encased in them. The center of long window made of glass can be found in luxury residences after Tongguang period. The center is mostly crabapple with rhombus shape patterned. During late Qing and the early Republican period there is window that is completely made of glass even including the skirt board section. The center for these windows still has patterns like crabapple with rhombus shape, which is distinctive from modern glass windows. These types of window can be found at Zhang's residence on Dongbei Street, and Wu's residence at Dashitou Alley. The carving on skirt board and Jiatangban can be simple line carving, or be carved with scenery, people, flower, or even ancient utensils. This depends on the finance and social environment when the piece was made. The carving technique and pattern both play a major role in identifying the period when the building is constructed. Long windows open to the outside if there is no attached passageway. The outside facing skirt board is complemented with exterior skirt board to prevent wind and rain, and carving can only be found on the interior side. Long windows open to the inside when there is a passageway attached to the outside of the building with the exception of some cases found in late period construction. The skirt boards are carved on both sides, and there is no exterior skirt board. The floor window opens to the outside when there is no exterior attached passageway. The buildings with attached passageway use awning windows more frequently. There can be railings beneath floor windows. Rain boards are attached to these railings to protect the area from rain.

玻璃、葵式嵌玻璃、花结嵌玻璃、八角锦嵌玻璃等。同光以后，豪华住宅其长窗心仔有衬玻璃，而心仔以海堂凌（菱）角为多。迄于晚期（清末民国初）有全部配玻璃者，甚至裙板部分也易玻璃，不过仍用海堂凌（菱）角心仔（非如今日之大玻璃窗），如东北街张宅、大石头巷吴宅等。至于夹堂板、裙板上之雕刻，有仅刻线脚，有刻山水、人物、花鸟及博古图案等，视财力而定，各时期均具特征。其雕刻手法及形式内容，均为考订建造年代之重要依据。长窗开启，一般建筑无外廊者皆向外开，其裙板朝外面有避风雨之外裙板，故裙板之雕刻则向内。建筑物有外廊者，长窗向内开，唯至后期亦有例外的，其裙板两面雕刻，不施外裙板。地坪窗于无外廊之建筑向外开，并加外裙板；在有外廊之建筑，多数用和合窗。地坪窗下为栏杆，栏杆外装雨挞板，以避风雨。

上：东北街张宅槅扇（门）
下左：阊门某宅大门

Top: Lattice doors of Zhang's residence on Dongbei Street
Bottom left: Main gate of a residence at Gate Chang

对页下右：铁瓶巷任宅装修
本页：铁瓶巷任宅东花厅

Opposite bottom right: Decoration of Ren's residence at Tieping Alley
This page: East flower hall of Ren's residence at Tieping Alley

铁瓶巷任宅东花厅槅扇（门）

Lattice doors of east flower hall of Ren's residence at Tieping Alley

大石头巷吴宅花厅槅扇（门）

Lattice doors of flower hall of Wu's residence at Dashitou Alley

上：卫道观前潘宅木漏窗（槅扇窗）
下：大石头巷吴宅楼厅槅扇（门）

Top: Wooden lattice window of Pan's residence at Weidaoguanqian
Bottom: lattice doors of storied hall at Wu's residence at Dashitou Alley

上：庙堂巷畅园留云山房装修
下：王洗马巷万宅楼厅支摘窗

Top: Decoration of Liuyunshanfang of Changyuan Garden
Bottom: Sustained (awning) window of storied hall of Wan's residence at Wangxianma Alley

王洗马巷万宅花厅装修

Decoration of flower hall of Wan's residence at Wangxianma Alley

景德路某宅槅扇（窗）

Lattice windows of a residence on Jingde Road

上：景德路杨宅楼厅装修
左下：铁瓶巷顾宅装修
右下：铁瓶巷顾宅（藏书楼）槅扇（门）

Top: Decoration of storied hall of Yang's residence on Jingde Road
Bottom left: Decoration of Gu's residence at Tieping Alley
Bottom right: Lattice door of library building of Gu's residence at Tieping Alley

韩家巷鹤园花厅小窗

Small window of flower hall of Crane Graden

栏杆　栏杆有装于走廊两柱之间，有装于地坪窗、和合窗之下。低者称"半栏"，上设坐槛者又称"栏凳"。坐槛及栏凳有木制，亦有用砖与雕空方砖，很雅洁，又有以预制玻璃瓦件作栏板的。木制栏杆其花纹以万川、乱纹、回文、笔管为多。半栏有上加吴王靠，可资憩坐。南石子街潘宅，楼层走廊栏杆内外两层，内木制者较高，外铁制者较低，花纹为新式，因该处并作女宾观剧之用，两栏之夹层为弃置果壳杂物之用。该建筑年代晚近，充分反映封建贵族阶层享乐之生活。

天花　李斗《工段营造录》云："吴人谓罳顶，……所以使屋不呈材也。"在苏州旧住宅中甚少见。马大箓巷邱宅花厅尚见方形格支条糊纸天花一例。江南夏季炎热，屋顶施草架覆水椽，室内空间高畅，隔热效果亦好。李渔《一家言·居室部》所谓："常因屋高檐矮，意欲取平，遂抑高者就下，顶格（天花）一概齐檐，使高蔽有用之区，委之不见不闻。"此正苏州旧住宅天花罕见之因。

Railing

Railings are used between columns of covered passages and are called Langan, underneath awning or floor windows. The short railing is called half railing, and railing seats have a horizontal piece for seating. Railing seats can be made from wood, brick, or hollowed square brick. The boards of railings can be made from fabricated glazed tiles. Wood railings have patterns like Wanchuan, random line, Huiwen (palindrome), and writing brush. A Wuwangkao is set at the half railing for comfort seating. At Pan's residence on Nanshizi Street, the railing along a upper story exterior passage has two sections. The inner section is made of wood and taller, and the outside section is shorter and made of metal with new patterns. This area is used for ladies to enjoy opera, and the crevice formed by the two sections of railing is used as a dump for peels and seeds of melons and fruits. This building in Pan's residence is relatively modern, and reflects the living style of aristocrats during that period.

Ceiling

The book *Gongduan Yingzao Lu* by Li Dou notes, "The Wu people calls it Siding, ... hides the roof frame from viewing." This is not a widely adopted practice in traditional Suzhou houses. The flower hall of Qiu's residence at Madalu Alley using square frames with glued paper ceiling is one prime example. It is hot during summer months in this region and a rough frame with double ceiling is bestowed on the roof to increase the internal height of rooms. This technique improves heat insulation. In the Chapter of Residences of *Yijiayan*, Li Yu stated, "Due to the difference in high building and low eaves, to produce a uniform surface it is necessary to suppress the tall part. The ceiling are uniformly placed at the level of the eave, and hides the functional part that need to be tall, so they can not be seen or heard." This is the reason why ceiling is rarely found in Suzhou.

南石子街潘宅楼层

Upper story of Pan's residence on Nanshizi Street

上：小新桥巷刘宅耦园栏杆
下：东北街张宅坐凳栏杆

Top: Railing of Ouyuan Garden
Bottom: Railing seats of Zhang's residence on Dongbei Street

上：东北街张宅楼层栏杆
下：西百花巷程宅楼层栏杆

Top: Upper story railing of Zhang's residence on Dongbei Street
Bottom: Upper story railing of Cheng's residence at Xibaihua Alley

石作　石料有金山石、焦山石、青石及绿豆石等。金焦二石俱花岗岩，出苏城之西南。青石产洞庭西山，属石灰岩，苏州早期住宅皆用此。绿豆石属砂石一种。乾嘉以后金山石大量采用。青石质细宜于施工，雕刻效果好。至于冰裂纹铺地取青石及黄石，甚雅且洁，易自由拼合。

木料　苏州为水乡，近无高山，故建筑所用木料十之八九仰求于他省，如福建、江西、浙江等地。苏州旧住宅所用木材，杉木品种有西木，产于江西；广木，产于湖广（湖南、湖北）；建木，产于福建。明代住宅则以楠木为多，今所谓"楠木大厅"者。木材因仰之于水运，皆先以一定尺度断料，建筑高度遂受到一定的限制，故苏州"叉柱"之法，得能不衰，仍赓续使用，而卯榫制作特精。余调查宋构三清殿，其柱用"叉柱"。黄杨木、银杏木附近兼有少量出产，用于华丽的装修及若干局部。木表髹漆：柱黑色退光，梁枋用栗色，挂落用墨绿，屏门用白色。此皆与江南较炎热气候相关而采用素雅色彩。

Stone

The various types of stone as construction materials include Jinshanshi（金山石）, Jiaoshanshi（焦山石）, Qingshi（青石 or black stone) and Lüdoushi（绿豆石）etc. Jin and Jiao hills, located southwest of Suzhou, produce granites. Black stone, which is widely used in early building periods, is a kind of limestone from West Dongting Hill. Lüdoushi is a type of sandstone. After Qianlong and Jiaqing period Jinshanshi became widely adopted in construction. Black stone is fine and easy to be modfied and carved. For ice break pattern floor black and yellow stone are used. Black and yellow stone is clean, classy, and easy to conjoin.

Lumber

Suzhou is a city with streams and lakes. There is no nearby mountain or hill as a source for wood. Over eighty percent of the lumber used in building construction comes from locations like Fujian, Jiangxi, and Zhejiang provinces. A type of Shanmu called Ximu comes from Jiangxi. Guangmu is produced in today's Hunnan, Hubei provinces, and Jianmu can be found in Fujian. Residences constructed during Ming dynasty mostly use Nanmu. This is what forms the so-called Nanmu Hall. Lumber is transported to Suzhou via rivers, which limits the length of lumber and height of the building as well. The forking column（叉柱）technique makes it possible to increase the building height. This technique refined over a long period of time has brought a fine skill in the making of joint. The Sanqingdian structure built during Song dynasty that I surveyed uses the forking column technique in its columns. Huangyang（黄杨）and gingko can be found in small quantities locally. These types of lumber are used for elaborate decorations, and some small constructions. The lumber is all covered with enamel. Columns are enameled in flat black, roof frames in brown chestnut color, flying panels are dark green, and screen doors are white. These soft colors are used due to the warm climate in this region.

Trees and Flowers

The method of placing trees and flowers in a garden along with hillocks and ponds is discussed along with theory of garden building. In general the residential courtyard grounds are paved with stone slabs, or various stone patterns. The general consideration in courtyard layout is that the ground should be elegant-looking, easy to clean, fast drying, and hard for weeds to grow. It is also important to maximize open space. This makes it easy to conduct various activities outside the building, which is one of the advantages of buildings with individual yards. The flowerbeds are lined with bricks, or stones that are used to build hillocks. A few rocks are placed and a couple of banana trees or bamboo trees are planted at the corner. The planting of trees is to accomplish three purposes. First, trees can provide shades and a good airflow, and do not spoil the air circulation. The commonly planted trees are tall with few branches near the ground such as Chinese parasol and maple. These trees lose their leaves during the winter, allowing sunshine to come through and provide warmth for the rooms. Second, they can provide a light aroma if Jingyingui (金银桂), Yulan (玉兰) and Haitang (海棠) are planted together. These flowers, with Mudan (牡丹) in the flowerbeds compose a view of Yutangfugui (玉堂富贵 , means fortune in Chinese). Third is planting white bark pine in front of flower hall or studies because its shape is serene, the branches and leaves are loose, and it has the pose of a large tree. The book *Wufenglu* notes, "even the poor of this region still decorate a small pot of plants for enjoyment." This shows even during Song dynasty the residents of this area had a deep affection for plants and trees. In addition to trees and flowers planted in the courtyard, the potted plants are always altered as the residents like.

花木配置　庭园栽植，其布置方法用叠山凿池则于园林论中及之。普通在住宅天井中以石板铺地、花街铺地，总从地面雅洁、宜于淋扫、易于干燥、少长杂草等多方面考虑，并且还要达到扩大空间面积，在室外可作生活活动的目的，此为院落式住宅优点之一。天井中有用砖筑花坛，有用假山石叠花坛，间有置一二峰石，墙角栽芭蕉一丛，或植修竹数竿。植树之目的有三：第一，能遮炎日，而又要通风良好，且不阻碍地面空间流通。所选树种以梧桐、青枫、树槐之类等干高、下部枝叶少者，至冬季时落叶，满院煦阳，得以取暖，是能符合上项条件。第二，既能遮炎日又散清香，则用金银桂、玉兰、海棠共植，花坛中布置牡丹，谐音为"玉堂富贵"。第三，花厅、书斋前植白皮松，以其姿态古拙、枝叶松透、小树而寓大树之容。《吴风录》有云："……虽闾阎下户，亦饰小小盆岛为玩。"自宋人记载中已见到当时居民之爱好。因此，天井中除栽植植物外，亦有盆栽随时作更换之需要。

上：东北街拙政园明代门枕石
下：天官坊陆宅明代须弥座

Top: Stone block of Ming dynasty at gate of Zhuozheng Garden
Bottom: Carved base of Ming dynasty of Lu's residence at Tianguan Fang

上：东北街李宅花厅前铺地
下：碧凤坊金宅花园铺地

Top: Pattern-covered ground in front of flower hall of Li's residence on Dongbei Street
Bottom: Pattern-covered ground of garden of Jin's residence at Bifeng Fang

碧凤坊金宅花厅前绿化

Plants before flower hall of Jin's residence at Bifeng Fang

上：韩家巷鹤园花园东望
下：韩家巷鹤园花园西望

Top: Viewing Crane Garden from east
Bottom: Viewing Crane Garden from west

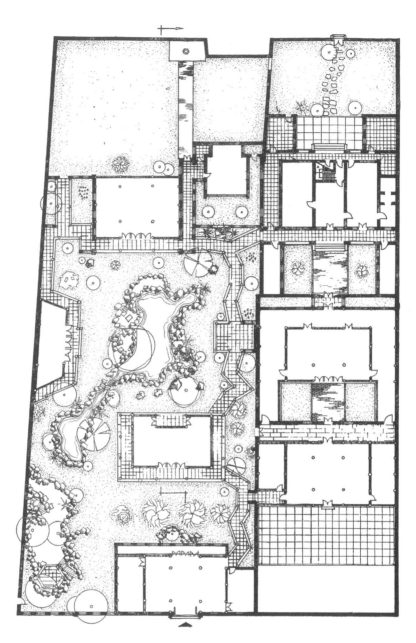

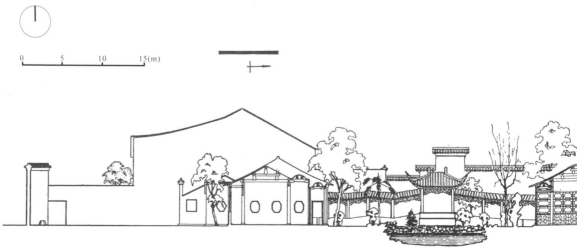

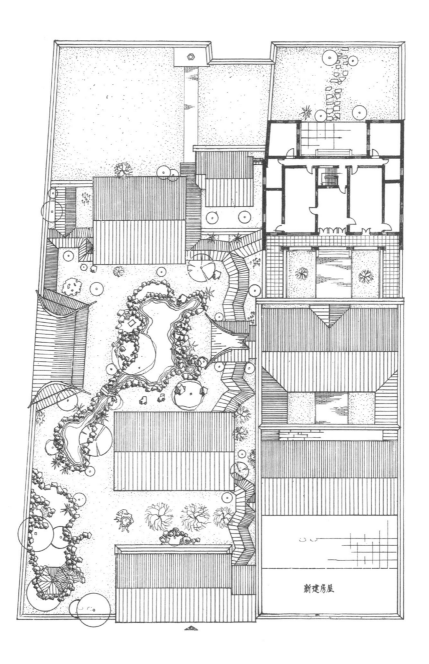

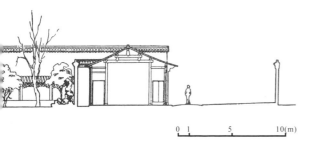

新建房屋

对页上：韩家巷鹤园一层平面图
本页上：韩家巷鹤园二层平面图
下：韩家巷鹤园剖面图

Opposite top: Ground floor plan of Crane Garden
This page top: First floor plan of Grane Garden
Cross page: Section of Crane Garden

0 1   5   10(m)

水井 在一般住宅中，少者一口，多者数口。有在天井中、厨房前或园中，更有在避弄中，或有于屋内作暗井（井口塥砖）。其他尚有街巷中公井。池中亦凿井以调节水源，对于养鱼亦多好处。天井中之大水缸，积檐漏而聚之，专供饮料兼作消防之用，称"天落水"。此种大水缸称"太平缸"。

排水 苏州河流纵横，对排水起了很大作用。住宅排水系在天井中筑阴井，大门前有总下水道。过去苏州坊巷皆铺石板，形式与宋《平江图》所示相符。石板下为下水道，路面修整清洁，范庄前用二横夹一道的铺法，吴人称其为"篦箕街"。近日在旧平江府子城遗址前掘出砖塥路面，其下之下水道亦为砖砌，极完整宽阔。

Water Well

There is at least one well in each residence. The wells can be located in courtyard, in front of kitchen, in gardens, or even in Bilong area. There is also hidden well that are covered with bricks inside buildings. Public wells can be found along roads. The water pounds can have well dug underneath to improve water circulation. This is beneficial for fishes that are kept in these pounds. Large porcelain containers are placed in courtyards to collect water from rain fall and roof run-offs. These are used for drinking as well as fire fighting. The water collected are called "sky dropped water" (天落水), and the water vessels are called "safety vessels" (太平缸).

Drainage

The waterways in Suzhou play a important role in drainage. The residences have hidden gutters underneath courtyard for draingage. There drains are collected and fed into a main gutter in front of the main gate. Streets are covered with stone slabs in a style that matches those shown in the *Map of Pingjiang* drawn during Song dynasty. The drainage is located underneath the slabs. This gives an orderly view from outside. The street at Fanzhuangqian (范庄前) has slabs laid in a pattern that one vertical slab is sandwiched between two horizontal. This is the so-called Biqijie (篦箕街 , comb street) in this area. The recently excavated brick covered street at the remains of Zi Cheng (子城 , a small city) of old Pingjiang Fu has brick laid drainage system. This drainage system with wide drains is extremely well preserved.

纽家巷太平天国英王府（旧潘宅）纱帽厅前
Garden in front of gauze hat hall of Prince Ying's Mansion (Pan's
residence at Niujia Alley)

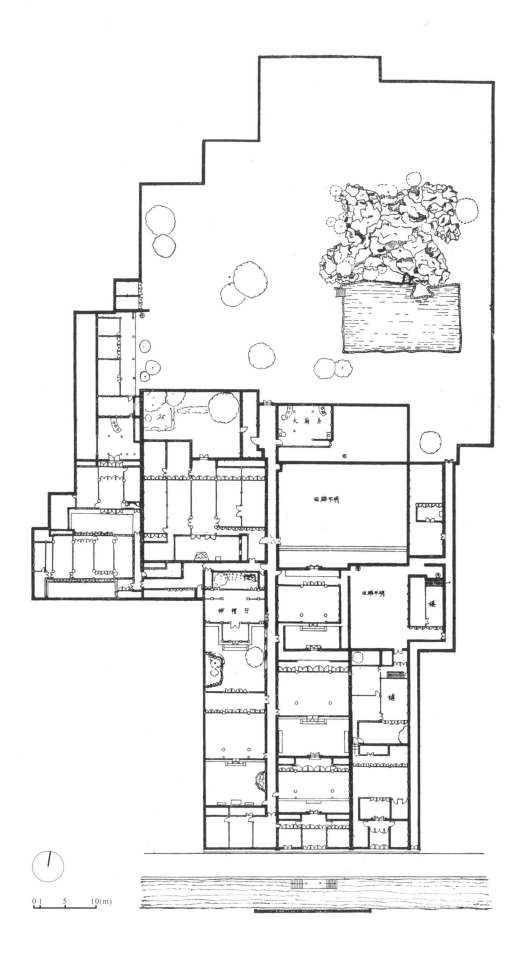

大厨房

旧跡不明

旧跡不明

轿帽厅

楼

楼

0 1　　5　　10(m)

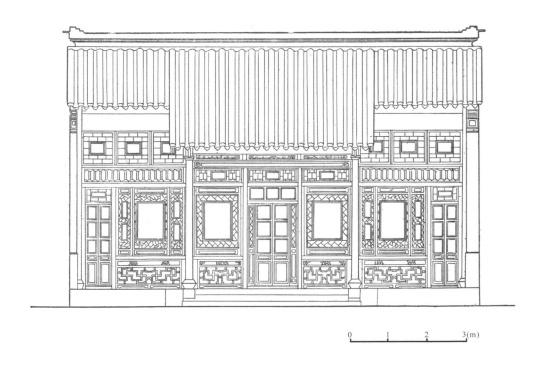

0　　　1　　　2　　　3(m)

对页：纽家巷太平天国英王府（旧潘宅）平面图
本页上：纽家巷太平天国英王府纱帽厅（旧潘宅）立面图
本页下：苏州旧坊巷石板铺路

Opposite: Floor plan of Prince Ying's Mansion (Pan's residence at Niujia Alley)

This page top: Elevation of gauze hat hall of Prince Ying's Mansion (Pan's residence at Niujia Alley)

This page bottom: Stone paving of an old lane of Suzhou

范庄前街巷景

View of the lane at Fanzhuangqian

砂皮巷入口巷景

View of the entrance of Shapi Alley

苏州旧住宅以建筑风格论，明末清初之秀挺简洁，清乾隆嘉庆时之雄健厚重，同治光绪后之精巧华丽，皆为鉴定建筑年代之总着眼处。明末清初退休官僚以苏州为"颐养"之地，固多营建。清乾嘉时，大官僚地主以当时充沛财力物力续造大住宅。同光以后多数以镇压太平天国农民革命起家之官僚又集苏州，踵事增华，遂使苏州旧式大住宅遗存至多。因而，此成为今日研究古代建筑之重要实例。

To sum up the general features of the traditional Suzhou residences, conclusions are made that the residences in late Ming and early Qing dynasties are elegant and eminent; those in Qianlong and Jiaqing periods are grand and massive; and in Tongzhi and Daoguang periods they are refined and luxurious. These features are essential to identify the age of the construction. To be detailed, residences in late Ming and early Qing dynasties are mainly constructed by the retired government officials for their rest of life; those in Qianlong and Jiaqing periods are residences of powerful officials and squires; and in Tongzhi and Daoguang periods, those officials who beated down the Taiping Tianguo uprising group gathered here to construct more buildings. That is why there are so many grand buildings remained till present days. They are important and vivid samples for the scholars to study the traditional constructions.

附记 | Excursus

一九五八年九月余编《苏州旧住宅参考图录》梓行,曾撰《苏州旧住宅》一文,宣读于十月间北京建筑工程部建筑科学院所召开之学术讨论会,当时所发油印本,今几无存,因索者众,爰将此付刊,并为《苏州旧住宅参考图录》之解说。

一九八〇年一月陈从周记于同济大学建筑系

I compiled *Pictures and Figures of Traditional Suzhou Residences* and had it printed in Sep. 1958. Besides, I wrote an article titled "Traditional Suzhou Residences" and read it out in the seminar held in Beijing by the Institute of Architecture Science of the Ministry of Architecture and Construction. The handouts at that time were mimeographed and few of them were left today, so I have the article published, enclosed with illustration of those pictures and figures, to meet the demands of readers.

Chen Congzhou

Architecture Department of Tongji University

Jan. 1980

图书在版编目（CIP）数据

苏州旧住宅：纪念版 = Traditional Suzhou Residences（Centenary Edition）：
中文、英文 / 陈从周著 . -- 上海：同济大学出版社，2018.11
ISBN 978-7-5608-8167-6

Ⅰ . ①苏… Ⅱ . ①陈… Ⅲ . ①民居—建筑艺术—苏州—图集
Ⅳ . ① TU241.5-64

中国版本图书馆 CIP 数据核字 (2018) 第 219584 号

苏州旧住宅

陈从周 著

英文翻译：陈威 陈水英　　摄影：陈从周
封面摄影原作：苏州市房产管理局（《苏州古民居》，2004）
书名与题字书法：乐峰

出 版 人　　华春荣
责任编辑　　罗璇 武蔚
责任校对　　张德胜
装帧设计　　博风建筑

出版发行　　同济大学出版社　　http://www.tongjipress.com.cn
　　　　　　地址：上海市四平路 1239 号　　邮编：200092　　电话：021-65985622
经　　销　　全国各地新华书店
印　　刷　　上海丽佳制版印刷有限公司
开　　本　　787mm×1092mm　　1/16
印　　张　　15
字　　数　　374 000
版　　次　　2018 年 11 月第 1 版　　2021 年 12 月第 2 次印刷
书　　号　　ISBN 978-7-5608-8167-6
定　　价　　85.00 元